MW00810892

"JUST GIMME A ZERO!"

(Teaching From the Trenches)

By

Mary Jack Edwards

Illustrations
By
Christopher Edwards Ingle

For Sue,

Now you'll know how hard I've been working all these years! You're a dear friend and we have had some good times —

Love,

Mary Jack

"Just Gimme A Zero!"

(Teaching From The Trenches)

Layout and design: Ray Campbell
Illustrations: Christopher Edwards Ingle
Cover art: Mike Sigurdson

Copyright © 1999 by Mary Jack Edwards

Additional copies of this book may be purchased by contacting the publisher:

Ringtail Productions Limited
P.O. Box 141084
Irving, Texas, 75014

ISBN-0-9617487-2-9

Printed by Taylor Publishing Company
Dallas, Texas

First printing: June, 1999

CONTENTS

Dedication
Acknowledgments
Foreword
Preface — What Teachers Have to Say

*This book is dedicated to
the most important profession
in our society...the teaching profession.
Without teachers, there would be
no other professions*

ACKNOWLEDGMENTS

My sincere thanks to those who contributed to the book. Teachers were given the opportunity to express their views and their quotations are found in italic print throughout the book on a variety of subjects. Their names were changed to protect their privacy. Any familiar name is purely coincidental.

Special technical and production assistance thanks to my two anonymous readers, Ray Campbell for the layout and design, Jack Lynch of Commercial Printing for collateral printing needs and Jay Love of Love and Associates, Incorporated for printing coordination.

My appreciation to friends and family who encouraged me to keep writing when I was discouraged and frustrated.

A special thank you to Carol Sue Pier, whose contributions helped make this book possible. Carol, an outstanding high school teacher, left the profession in May, 1996. She had "had enough." Teachers like Carol cannot be replaced.

The cover for the book is by a talented young artist, Mike Sigurdson, who taught across the hall from me. His artistic talent is superb and his financial compensation as a teacher is so low that I am sure education will lose him.

I am grateful to Mike and Judy Howard for their support and their friendship at a time when I really needed it. Their belief in the book and their enthusiasm to get it published gave me the determination I needed to bring it to completion.

To my late parents, Mary and Jack Edwards, my deep love and gratitude. They gave me a loving home and always stressed the importance of an education and worked very hard to pay for mine. How lucky I was to have had them for my parents.

And to my sons Christopher Edwards Ingle and Paul Ingle Jr., my sincere thanks to them both.

Christopher was the cartoonist for the book and his artistic talent never ceases to amaze me. His encouragement is deeply appreciated.

Paul is the one who convinced me this book should be written to let the public know the truth about public education and that I was the one who could do it. His faith in me has been a blessing.

And to my dear friend Jo...in loving memory.

FOREWORD

Over the last few months, I have read *"Just Gimme A Zero!"* *(Teaching From the Trenches)* at least four times. With each reading, two observations were noted: most of the information in the book seemed very familiar, and most of the information detailing problems with public schools had never seen the light of day in printed form. And it was this last point that made the decision easy to publish Mary Jack Edwards' insightful look at public education from the vantage point of a real battle-scared teacher in the trenches.

While most readers of this book will nod their heads in agreement *(teachers and parents)* with the assessments documented, there will be others *(particularly bureaucrats and elected politicos)* who will wince at the boldness of the assertions stated. And why is this? The reason is simple...too many school bureaucrats and elected officials who have the power and ability to effect changes in public education are more interested in creating fiefdoms, promoting "new" programs, maintaining the status quo or "rubber stamping" the actions of others all in the name of educational progress. Attend any local school board or state education committee meeting and witness the truthfulness of this assertion.

Until parents (even those without children in school) and teachers make a genuine commitment to become actively involved in all aspects of running, monitoring and participating in the work of making the schools in their community a priority, the picture of the final product being released from schools in today's society will remain bleak.

Over the course of years examining public education in my community, I have observed that there are two matters an entrenched educational bureaucrat or elected politico fears the most: 1) letters or articles in local newspapers that provide an objective or truthful perspective on the inane or blundering activities of these "powers-that-be" *(whether hired or elected)*; and 2) the appearance of actively involved parents and teachers before boards and commissions to express their dismay by pointing out the folly of the actions perpetrated by these individuals.

However, therein lies part of the problem. Not enough parents and teachers — the front line forces for real reform in the education trenches — devote enough time or attention to the processes that will shape the lives of our future generations.

And many participants who do take time often have a "specific" agenda to accomplish that may or may not be for the betterment of the entire educational process.

If medical science could ever develop a pill or vaccination to eliminate public apathy or cure the reluctant attitude of all parents and teachers by making them fully involved, then, just maybe, we would witness a re-birth of learning, a system that works for all students and yes, a system where fewer "zeros" would be apathetically accepted.

Until this day of active enlightenment arrives and everyone is "vaccinated" with a renewed concern to participate in the educational processes of their communities, we will have to be content with brave troopers in the trenches like Mary Jack Edwards who wage the battle on our behalf. And wouldn't it be great if we could recognize these teaching veterans in the manner that they should be recognized...with respect, dignity, compensation and gratitude?

Mike E. Howard
President
Ringtail Productions Limited

PREFACE

ON TEACHING "Teaching is more complex and multifaceted than most adults realize, because they are basing their beliefs on school as they knew it."

ON STUDENTS "Students today are apathetic and 'me oriented.' They are aimless, lonely, unhappy and lack ambition, self-esteem and confidence."

ON PARENTS "I don't know what parents are doing as far as parenting is concerned. They certainly are not teaching basic social skills, self-discipline, respect, manners, or the value of an education. I am thankful for those parents who are caring and helpful toward their children and logical when it comes to dealing with teachers."

ON CURRICULUM "We are given so much to cover in one year and expected to spend a large part of the day on preparing for THE TEST. I always feel like I'm dancing as fast as I can!"

ON DISCIPLINE "Teachers are frustrated and I am sure administrators are too. If there is no discipline in the home, we must spend a major part of our class time trying to discipline disruptive students. You are not encouraged to take a stand because you must 'cover your ass.' Students get by with a lot more than they should."

ON SALARIES "In our society, respect is generally connected with earning power. Teacher earning power is still a joke and teachers certainly are not respected."

ON EVALUATIONS "They require teachers to perform, rather than teach. Some who cannot teach, can perform."

ON MORALE "It is at an all-time low. Every year we are given more and more responsibility. The negative is emphasized and the millions who receive a good education are not news. Teachers are fed up and burned out!"

ON TEST SCORES "News flash! Test scores do not measure student learning and never did! Yet we are expected to spend valuable time on preparing for testing because THEY *(and THEY know who they are)* say so. THEY don't know what they are talking about. To rate a child's learning and the success rate of a school by one stupid test is insane!"

ON SCHOOL SAFETY "In the violent world we live in today, it is ridiculous to believe that schools are safe places. Have you listened to the news lately? Students are not safe with each other and faculties are not safe with certain students. Wake up America! We are fighting a war in our public schools!"

ON TEACHERS "There is a tremendous shortage of teachers now, but we haven't seen anything yet! Teachers are leaving the profession by the thousands in every state...the experienced teachers and the new ones, too!"

ON THE FUTURE "There are solutions to the problems and there is hope. There has to be for the survival of our nation. There must be a decision made whether public schools are going to continue to be social agencies and battlefields, or places to learn."

Chapter One
The Good Old Days

BEASTS OF BURDEN

$1,300 a day

$122.50 a day

$222.50 a day

$2,000 a day

REMEMBER THE GOOD OLD DAYS?

Some people say there were no "good old days." I say there *were* some good old days and I remember them. This was the time before "the pill" when safe sex was only a lock on the bedroom door.

AIDS was a diet candy. People came out of their closets, but this didn't mean they were announcing their sexual preference. When we said we were gay, we meant we were happy; and if something was bad it meant something was lousy.

Only women wore earrings and ponytails and the men wore suits and ties. We mowed our "grass" and "pot" was something we cooked in. Coke was a popular soft drink and wasn't sniffed up the nose, while "crack" was what we jumped over on the sidewalk so we wouldn't "break our mother's back."

The only socially acceptable way for a man and woman to live together openly was preceded by a wedding. Childbirth out of wedlock was not something to advertise. And a person's reputation, integrity and honesty was of the utmost importance.

We knew our neighbors, and children played safely outside after dark. A drive-by was just that...driving by with maybe a wave or a honk, but never with a spray of bullets. Everyone could honk his/her car horn while driving without the fear of being shot. Car-jacking referred to jacking-up a car to change a flat tire. Home security consisted of a front door lock.

The intimate details of the sex life of the President of the United States and other politicians were not discussed in newspapers, magazines or on radio and television. Good taste did not refer to food.

And in the good old days parents took responsibility for their children. There was no big discussion on the lack of values and manners because most parents taught them and children learned them.

When we sent our children to school this was considered a safe place for them to be. If a kid got a spanking at school for misbehaving, more often than not, he/she got one at home, too. Teachers were respected and admired and they were treated with adoration and dignity by both students and parents. Why, who would ever imagine the possibility of teachers getting dressed like everyone else, or indulging in mundane pursuits like eating, sleeping, shopping or soaking their feet?   Teachers actually seemed different from everyone else. And they were. **They were teachers, for heaven's sake!**

Do you remember when students went to school and were expected to be respectful, responsive and responsible along with learning the other three R's? Remember when kids were held accountable for their own performance and behavior by both teachers and parents? The result, of course, allowed teachers to teach and students to learn. That was, after all, what school was all about.

In the good old days, an education, our public schools and our teachers were highly important aspects in our lives.   All three of them ranked right up there at the top on everybody's list. Society knew the value of a good education. Talking back to a parent or teacher, or heaven forbid cursing one, was as unheard of as walking on the moon. Whatever happened to "children should be seen and not heard?"

During the good old days, children marched off to school carrying books and notebooks with pens and pencils and perhaps a sack lunch, but not with backpacks, guns and knives or perhaps a stash of drugs. Discipline problems consisted of chewing gum, talking and passing notes. The really serious behavior problem was carving initials on desks. Only those "rowdy boys" did such a thing!

Classrooms across America were not filled with students from a variety of cultures who could not speak the English language. Those students who came to America from other countries managed to learn the language on their own, usually by hearing it spoken at school. Their parents were eager to learn English as well because they were proud to be contributing citizens of this country.

Public school teachers were not expected to put up with — much less teach — disruptive, disrespectful or dangerous students, or those with severe learning, emotional or behavioral problems. Classes were not jammed to overcrowding, habitual absenteeism was rare, and drug abuse was nonexistent.

Teachers didn't spend their valuable time teaching everything from basic manners to the rest of all the social skills including the difference between right and wrong, or all the other traditional values. Kids came to school knowing these things because they were taught at home. Home is where they should be taught. Teachers were never meant to be both parent and teacher.

Parents were supportive of teachers and teachers were allowed to do the job they were hired to do...teach. Teachers were in control of their own classroom and determined what did and did not go on there. It is hard today to even imagine teaching in such a situation.

Teachers weren't required to put on a circus-style "dog and pony show" to prove over and over again that they could indeed teach. They didn't have to spend hours trying to climb out from under piles of unnecessary paperwork. Although the school bureaucracy was alive and well then, it was only the size of a pin head compared to today's bureaucratic monstrosity.

Standards and expectations were kept at high levels...period. Standards were not adjusted to accommodate students, but students adjusted to accommodate standards and expectations.

Today, we adjust standards to accommodate students meaning we have adjusted ourselves to the lowest standards ever seen in public schools. And expectations? Teachers begin every school year with high expectations and the idea that "this year will be different." But it seldom is different. And very often it is worse than the year before.

I can just hear legislators, school boards and school administrators all over the nation saying, "That's not true! Public schools have not lowered their standards!" Well it is true. And if you don't believe it, ask a public school teacher. Or better yet, ask a college teacher or an employer.

Teachers today who try to maintain the same high standards set for their students five or ten years ago find themselves fighting an exhausting and futile daily battle with very few students passing and furious parents, principals and coaches.

Achievement tests were given once a year in the good old days. However, the most important evaluation of student performance and behavior was the teacher's grade book and the report card. And grades did not have to be changed by teachers or administrators to appease parents, or to have an acceptable percentage of passing and failing grades. School administrations will tell you this doesn't happen today either, but it does.

Nobody got "up tight" about yearly achievement testing. This test was very important, but it was just a test taken over

4

material students had spent the year learning. And everybody did their best and that was that.

Does anyone know what happened to the importance of the teacher's grade book?

Academics in the good old days never took a back seat to anything...especially to extra curricular activities. Sports and having a good time was very important, but second only to academics. "No pass no play" was unheard of. If you didn't pass, you couldn't play anything. And you probably wouldn't be able to sit down either! You were expected to pass — period, exclamation point.

And not once, in the good old days, did teachers pick up a newspaper or magazine and read that public school educators were doing a poor job and that it was their fault if Johnny or Joanie couldn't read or do math. If they couldn't read or do math problems it was their own fault, certainly not the teacher's fault. An education was there for them, and believe it or not, it still is today.

If Johnny and Joanie can't read or if they have low math scores today, the public is led to believe it is either because we aren't teaching reading and math correctly or we need new teaching techniques. Teachers are sent scurrying around in all directions to hear about someone's new innovative reading or math ideas for which the school district has paid big bucks. But most of the time, the perception is given that it's the teacher's fault. One thing for sure, it's never portrayed as being the student's fault.

Teachers in the good old days weren't given new teaching techniques to try as often as they changed their underwear. And while they didn't have the teaching tools of technology and the equipment we have today, they were still able to give their students a good education. Kids actually learned to read and write. They learned to spell and write complete sentences. They learned to add, subtract, multiply and divide. And without a calculator in sight!

Students learned to speak the English language without courses in "English As A Second Language." They learned enough to graduate from high school, enter college if they wanted to and become anything they wanted to be.

Those who didn't go on to college had learned enough to enter the job market and become productive citizens.

Were kids smarter than they are today? Of course not. They just did what they were supposed to do. And they had some of the same problems, hurts, difficulties, hard times and disappointments young people have had since the beginning of time. But they knew that nobody was going to take care of them but themselves and they needed an education to survive. They also had basic pride and self-respect...two attributes that are essential to the human condition. Where did they get these basic attributes? For the most part at home along with a little expansion and encouragement by their teachers. Well, things have changed.

Today, students in our public schools are **bribed**. Bribed to read, behave, complete assignments, make passing grades and attend school regularly.

In one school in grades 7-12 each A earned $40, a B earned $20, and a C earned $10. Business groups funded the program and the money was held in escrow until high school graduation. The money could be used for college or vocational training. A student who earned all A's in the seventh to the twelfth grade could receive $4,800. This is considered an incentive, not a bribe. There is nothing wrong in trying to motivate students to study and further their education. As we all know, money is a big motivation.

However, incidences of bribery have bordered on the ridiculous as these examples note:

- Schools offer pizza, ice cream, hot-dogs and popcorn parties for regular attendance. *(School finance is based on school attendance, you see.)*

- Motion pictures are shown on Fridays during school hours for students who have not misbehaved during the week.

- For good conduct or passing grades, other schools will reward students with cheeseburgers and drawings for radios, tape recorders, calculators and T-shirts.

- Even principals get in on the act. One principal dared his students to maintain a 96 percent attendance record for one month and in return he would have his head shaved. He lost the dare and his hair.

- As promised, another principal climbed the flag pole in front of her school because her students passed the standardized state test.

- The school roof is a popular place for bribery. One teacher stayed on the school roof all day and all night as a reward for increased school attendance; while another teacher sat on the roof of her school because her students read a certain number of books.

There are many more ways students are bribed, but the worst may be paying students money to attend school; get to school on time; bring their eye glasses, books, pens, pencils and paper to school; stay out of fights and behave in class. Schools aren't doing that, are they? Yes, they are. And a lot more!

What about all the students who work hard and do everything others are bribed to do? How do they feel? How would you feel?

In the future, will we see principals and teachers eating fire, walking over hot coals, or getting pies thrown in their faces in order to get students to do what they should be doing in the first place? No scheme they might try in public schools would surprise teachers.

What message are we sending students with these capers? Aren't we sending the message that in the real world they will be bribed to go to work every day, bribed to get along with their co-workers and bribed to do their job in the workplace?

If parents want to reward their kids for attending school, behaving, reading books, or passing tests, that's great. However, schools should demand that these things are done. Bribery is not the answer nor should it be public education's role to contribute to this expectation.

However, we can and we do teach work ethics, promptness, dependability, responsibility, loyalty, self-discipline, getting along with others and taking pride in accomplishment. Obviously, fewer kids are learning these things at home as they once were. Of course, these are all extra responsibilities added to the long list of others thrown at the classroom teacher who is expected to raise and parent children today. This, I might add, pushes academics back a notch further.

Although teachers must always continue to try to motivate, inspire and have high expectations for students' performance, it is unrealistic to believe that schools can do it alone and expect successful results. Parents have the ultimate responsibility to motivate and demand performance and responsibility from their own children.

Somewhere along the line we decided that public education — and teachers particularly — can do it all. Well, they can't. And they shouldn't be expected to try.

Until we come full circle and parents are once again parenting their children, schools cannot function properly, teachers cannot teach properly and students will not learn properly.

The good old days are gone. During that era we had the right idea and the only sane idea about raising and educating our children. Thankfully, we still have parents who know this and raise their children accordingly.

Will students once again attend school because they are supposed to do so and because it is the law in this country? Probably not, until they once again have respect for the law. And that is a whole other chapter and another can of worms!

Kids once behaved because they were taught to behave. They learned because they were expected to learn and teachers and parents put up with little nonsense. Kids weren't perfect by any means, but they acted like kids and not mini-terrorists. Society realized an education determined the future. The importance of an education was drummed into our heads by parents, grandparents and teachers. Certainly, nobody wanted to be called ignorant or uneducated.

Today, it is considered by some students to be "cool" if they make failing grades and get into trouble. Many kids don't even know what the word uneducated means. And if you tell them to look it up in the dictionary, they can't spell the word either. And if I only had a dollar for every time I have heard the words: "Well how do you expect me to look it up if I can't spell it?"

What has happened to our self-pride and self-discipline? Is it gone forever? Students today attend school if they feel like it. They arrive at school when they feel like it. They behave or misbehave when they feel like it. If they feel like it — and most don't — they complete their homework. And if they feel like it they might study for a test, but teachers don't count on it. More often than not, they just **don't feel like it.**

Do television, movies and video games have an influence on our children? Of course they do. No question about it. How could a daily dose of violence, murder, sex, hatred, immorality, indecency and antisocial behavior not affect them? And how many of them see these same things in their own daily personal lives? More than we could possibly imagine.

If a student feels the need to tell a teacher to "go to hell" they do. Many students go a step further and tell their teacher "go f— yourself." Yes, they do that, too. Can you even imagine saying such a thing to a teacher when you went to school?

It is not an embarrassment to some students to fail or be called ignorant; and they don't give a thought to contributing to the world they live in or contributing to the downfall of society. If you tell them that the most dangerous circumstance in a culture is ignorance and immorality, some don't understand a word you say and others will laugh in your face.

Another thing that makes them laugh is to tell them that one day very soon they will have to support themselves and they won't have the tools to do so. They don't look beyond their own noses to the future. Scary, isn't it?

If teachers from those good old days walked into the classrooms of today, they would be appalled at the changes in public schools. Talk about a twilight zone!

Just imagine Miss Pool, a teacher from the good old days...all dressed up in her starched blouse and full skirt with a white hanky tucked in her belt. Her hair is pulled back in a neat bun, pearl earrings are clamped to her earlobes and sensible shoes are on her feet. She smells so good...just like roses.

Miss Pool is always in control and enjoys the respect and admiration of everyone. In fact, although everybody is scared of her, they also love her. A hug from Miss Pool could keep you going for a week!

She smiles when she is pleased. If she is displeased, just one stern look with a raised eyebrow would bring tears to your eyes. Nobody wants to displease Miss Pool.

Now imagine inviting Miss Pool into today's classroom. Hold on to your bun, Miss Pool! You are in for a very bumpy ride!

She waits at her classroom door to greet her students as they arrive. The first thing she hears is, "Who are you and what are you doing here? You sure are old! How old are you, anyway?"

After spending several minutes trying to get the students quiet, she finds herself raising her voice higher and higher to be heard. Finally, she finds herself screaming, something she has never done before...didn't even know she could.

She raises her eyebrow and gives "the look" to Bobby who is talking to Jason and not listening to her. "Don't look at *me* like that! You aren't my teacher!" Poor Miss Pool doesn't know that Bobby who is mainstreamed into regular classes is emotionally disturbed, and these outbursts are to be handled with "time out" and with no aggressive behavior on the teacher's part. Bobby, however, has been known to become very aggressive himself and uses vile language on occasion. Miss Pool is now reeling in her sensible shoes.

After giving a short test she was told to give, Miss Pool discovers that only three students out of thirty have passed the test. "Did you study?" she asks. "No, we didn't!" They don't know why, just didn't want to or just didn't have time.

John and Emily arrive late to class. John overslept, as he often does, and Emily didn't want to come to school today, saying, "But my stupid mother made me come anyway!" Miss Pool's blouse is beginning to lose its starch and so is she.

Six classes and 180 students later, not only are Miss Pool's eyes wide with amazement, but her bun is drooping and both eyebrows are raised in a fixed position above glazed eyes.

She won't be back for a second day. She is shocked and horrified at what she has seen and heard. And later, as she contemplated the day, she realized that very little was the same as it once was. How can teachers possibly do this everyday? *And I didn't hug one student today,* she thought.

Miss Pool only saw the tip of the iceberg...

Putting your hands on a student today is taking a big chance, whether it be for hugging or some other reason. Sad, but true. There are many horror stories of teachers falsely accused of abusing students sexually or otherwise.

Spankings at school are becoming a thing of the past. The majority of schools have stopped this practice as punishment because of potential lawsuits. All that is left resembling discipline is serving detention, spending time in in-school suspension or attending an alternative school for a certain amount of time. None of these punishments seem to impress these kids one way or the other. They could care less. And they love to be suspended from school and sent home because they get to watch television or sleep all day.

We are seeing more and more kids who seem to be in charge and call all the shots in their family. They don't respect their parents and talk to them with blatant disrespect.

Had most of us from the good old days even entertained the thought of speaking to our parents in this manner, we would have been knocked into the middle of next week!

The facts are that the problem kids today — and there are thousands of them in classrooms in this country — don't know what the word respect means. And the last thing on their list is getting an education. They won't hesitate to talk back to teachers, try to argue with them, curse them and on occasion hit one, if the notion strikes them. They cheat and steal like professionals and they are not embarrassed or remorseful when the are caught.

These kids don't listen to their teacher, because they don't care. They don't follow directions, because they didn't listen. They don't have their books or supplies, because they forget them. They forget them because it isn't important to them.

They can't do their work, because they didn't listen, which brings us to the beginning of the cycle and the bottom line...**they don't care**. And this is the situation which teachers today are held accountable. It is a daily war and we are losing it. And yet, we all wonder why thousands and thousands of teachers are saying, *"Adios!"* to the teaching profession.

One of the few things today's teachers do have in common with those of yesteryear are low salaries with few benefits. This scenario remains constant.

The teaching profession is the most important profession in our society. Without it, there would be no other professions. How would people learn? Besides, where would kids stay all day? Think about that for a few minutes! However, this country has never afforded the teaching profession the financial compensation and respect it deserves.

Perhaps, it all started back when standards were different for teachers and the work expected of them paid very low wages. And don't forget, most of the teachers were women.

The following are the Rules for School Teachers from the Buckeye Farm News in 1915:

- You will not marry during the term of your contract.
- You are not to keep company with men.
- You must be home between the hours of 8 p.m. and 6 a.m. unless attending school functions.
- You may not loiter downtown in any of the ice cream stores.
- You may not travel beyond the city limits unless you have the permission of the chairman of the board.
- You may not ride in a carriage or automobile with any man unless he is your father or brother.
- You may not smoke cigarettes.
- You may not dress in bright colors.
- You must wear at least two petticoats.
- Your dresses must not be shorter than two inches above the ankle.
- You must keep the school neat and clean and sweep the floor every day and at least once a week mop with hot, soapy water; clean the blackboards at least once a day; and start fires at 7 a.m. so the room will by warm by 8 a.m.

Whew! How did they ever get their first teacher? And in what asylum did she end up?

Teacher's responsibilities have, of course, changed drastically. I can't remember the last time I had to start the fires at 7:00 a.m. at my school. Don't believe I ever did. I can loiter downtown in the ice cream store all night if I want to. I wear bright colors all the time and rarely wear a petticoat! I can keep company with men if I want to and I drive my own automobile. Not only did I marry, I also got a d-i-v-o-r-c-e during the school year.

In 1915, teachers accepted the treatment and low salaries they received because they had no recourse. Not so today...teachers have other alternatives and are dropping out of teaching like flies.

In 1999, one of the most blatant mistreatment of teachers is the practice of increasing the salaries of new teachers coming into the profession with increases up to 30%. And with a signing bonus to boot! At the same time, they are giving experienced teachers salary increases of 2% to 5%. And what about a contract signing bonus for them? Are you kidding? Not a chance. It seems to me that they have this practice backwards.

School districts must offer excellent beginning salaries to attract people into the profession. No question about that. And new hires will more than earn every penny they are paid. But before they sign on the dotted line it would be wise to investigate their earning potential in the future.

One example is a school district in Texas that pays higher salaries than most. With a Bachelors degree, a beginning teacher can earn a salary of $30,000. In this same district, a teacher with the same degree and 30+ years of experience is earning $40,000. The earning potential after 30+ years is a whopping increase of $10,000!

What an incentive for commitment to teaching for both the beginning teacher and the experienced teacher! Did all those in charge of compensation flunk Economics 101?

However, to put things in proper perspective...I read that zebras rent for $2,000 a day and a camel makes $1,300 a day. Depending on what tricks they do, dogs start at $500 a day. Well, I got to thinking...after twenty-eight years of teaching, I was paid a salary of $37,000 a year. I was required to teach 190 days during the year, not counting overtime or the after-hours school functions I was required to attend. Doing the math, I figure I made approximately $194.74 a day before taxes. I have a college degree and I also know some tricks those animals never even heard of. Well, I figure I made a tad less than a jackass makes!

Here are some additional thoughts on teacher's salaries from those in the trenches:

"Our pay in comparison with other professions is still unbeliev-able and nobody seems to really care. We have low morale, few, if any, benefits and everyone speaks for teachers, but teachers. The media makes a big deal out of every small raise we receive, but very little is said when years pass and we receive little or none. We never come close to breaking even with the increases in the cost of living." Jane L.

"Do I think I am paid adequately? Hell no! My salary should be in line with the difficulty of my job and its enormous value to society. Salaries are the biggest joke any career conscious person could ever witness." Rob I.

"When you look at the lives a teacher influences and all that goes into educating and preparing students for life, teaching is a very valu-able service. You can't find that service any other place. I wish every

teacher in America could walk out of school one fine day and say, 'Find somebody else to do what we do at the salary we were paid. Bring the parents, the school boards and the politicians in to teach.' They might last a day or two!" Peggy F.

"Nobody outside the teaching field could possibly know how draining a day of teaching actually is, or how much overtime can be involved. Overtime without pay, I might add." Barbara P.

"Each year, the paperwork grows deeper, the requirements become stiffer, the working time increases, the job is harder and the salary remains ridiculous. And each year I become less interested in teaching." Jim B.

"Teachers have one of the most important jobs in the nation, training future citizens and leaders. Yet a high school graduate with little responsibility can make more money, have a 40-hour week and go home with no papers to grade. We have summers off, you say? School begins earlier and earlier in the year and ends later and later. The time we do have is spent going to school, or working a second job, or simply trying to recuperate from months of grueling combat." Becky C.

"Teaching is a wonderful profession. If parents taught their children to behave and appreciate learning so we could teach, it would be rewarding. If we were paid like we should be it would also be rewarding. However, parents don't, we aren't, and it isn't." Irene M.

"In our society, respect is generally connected with earning power. Teacher earning power is a joke and teachers certainly are not respected." Jessica B.

"Many retired teachers are living at the poverty level, so I doubt they would consider the past the good old days. But at least they had respect, cooperation and the opportunity to focus on teaching. We have none of those things." Bob L.

REMEMBER?

Remember the teachers that taught you to read and write?

Remember the teachers that made you finally see the light?

Remember the teachers who dried your tears,

And took the time to calm your fears?

Remember the stern teachers you wished would just go away,

But were the ones who taught you the things you use today?

Teachers struggled and pushed to make you learn.

They didn't give up on you and showed their concern.

Remember the humorous teachers that made your days
brighter,

And the burdens of growing up just a little bit lighter?

The knowledge you possess came from teachers, you see.

They wanted for you the very best you could be.

Teachers are special for all that they do,

And how many of us ever said, "Thanks, I appreciate you!"

Chapter Two
Accountability

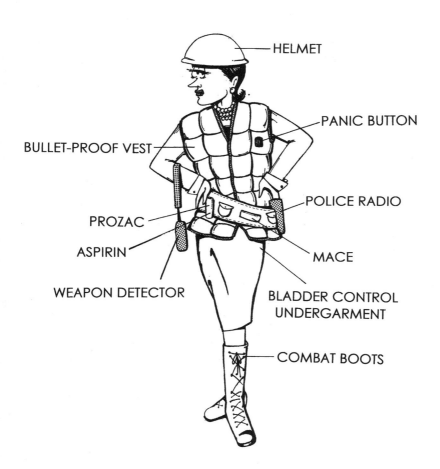

HELMET

PANIC BUTTON

BULLET-PROOF VEST

POLICE RADIO

PROZAC

ASPIRIN

MACE

WEAPON DETECTOR

BLADDER CONTROL
UNDERGARMENT

COMBAT BOOTS

FUTURE FACULTY FASHION

ACCOUNTABILITY

This book attempts to take the reader into the classroom of today and expose the impossible burden placed on our nation's teachers. While the public is constantly bombarded with the results of student's low test scores, absenteeism, dropping out, and those who are graduating with the inability to read, write, calculate and communicate, teachers themselves are bombarded with unreasonable demands and directives to solve all of these problems. And a multitude of others. When they cannot, it must be their fault and they are blamed once again.

As a public school teacher, I hope to provide some degree of insight into these and other significant problems regarding education. Through the years, as I have witnessed the tremendous changes in public education and have read about my profession and the problems that are constantly debated among the powers-that-be, I have often wished that somebody had asked my opinion or the opinions of my colleagues. Nobody ever did.

I have read absurd opinions and been given directives to implement that are unbelievable. Rarely have I seen the facts presented about what is going on in the classroom or have I seen workable solutions emerge from those opinions and directives.

Let me tell you about our schools, our students and especially about our teachers, who some believe are to blame for the big mess we call public education and yet are charged with the responsibility to fix it all.

The regular classroom teachers of today are expected to educate and meet the needs of the students who are: gifted, talented, above average, average, below average, disabled, mentally challenged, emotionally disturbed, multi-cultural non-English speaking, belligerent and dangerous. **And all in the same classroom!**

The United States is the only country in the world that tries to educate every single child with basically the same curriculum from kindergarten through high school. Could the rest of the world know something we have yet to figure out?

If we are sending students all the way through school

with a diploma they can't read and into the work force as poorly educated workers, who is to blame? Are teachers not doing their jobs? Shouldn't they be held accountable? If we are basing our opinion on schools as we knew them ten, twenty, thirty, or forty years ago, then the answer would probably be yes. If we are basing our opinion on first-hand knowledge of schools today, the answer would definitely be NO.

Whose fault is it anyway if Johnny and Sally simply refuse to learn? They occupy a chair in the classroom and that is the extent of their cooperation and efforts.

If Barbara and Jim have been in six other schools during the year and have little knowledge of a subject it is almost impossible to play catch-up even if they agree to try. The result is that they become a testing failure statistic.

And if Buster and Betty have spent more time in alternative school and in-school suspension for their behavior than they have in class, whose fault is it they haven't learned anything?

Then there are Jack and June who are habitually absent throughout the school year and whose parents are as apathetic as their children. They refuse to complete make-up work and consistently fail. Who is to blame for their lack of an education?

What about Dorothy and Don who are emotionally disturbed and a constant disruption in class? Not only do they not learn, they hinder the learning of others.

We are seeing a lot more of the Marys and Marks who are in school for only one reason. Attending school is a condition of parole. They are not interested in an education and no amount of effort on their teacher's part can change that. If they are not arrested for another offense, they will sit in their classes day in and day out, but that is all they will do... sit.

And last, but not least, what about the thousands and thousands of students in classrooms across this nation who do not want to be in school, don't care about an education and say they don't care, who refuse to pay attention, follow a simple direction, or complete an assignment? Should we hold their teachers accountable for their academic performance and test scores?

Should we hold teachers accountable for all these students collectively and base teacher evaluations and salaries on their performance? And should we base the success of an entire school on student test scores? Well, we do! And that isn't all, by a long shot.

Because standardized testing has become the way to judge student performance, it has also become the way to judge teacher performance and school performance. However, there are so many variables in a child's performance on one test and so much more involved in teaching than administering one test that using such a rating is ridiculous.

Today, preparing for and administering the latest standardized test has caused a feeding frenzy in our public schools. The test and those who put such value on it are the **PIRANHA** and the students and teachers are the **FEAST.**

Teachers are now forced to spend a large part of their teaching time drilling students for THE TEST and spending their conference period tutoring students to help them pass it. Students are pulled from their other classes for these tutoring sessions. And not only is the entire curriculum geared to this test, but so is the effectiveness and evaluation of both principals and teachers.

Is all of this nonsense time well spent in the classroom? Teachers and administrators certainly don't think so, with good reason, but they — the powers-that be — do think so and they are the ones who continue to make decisions concerning testing and a host of other things that greatly affect the teaching profession and the students.

In education, the popularity of individuals who make all these insane and inane decisions lies somewhere between The Third Reich, terrorists and very large hemorrhoids!

The general public and all those who profess to be leaders in this nation — beginning with the President of the United States and on down the line to state legislators and state and local school boards — don't have a clue what is going on in our public schools...not a clue! They don't know what teachers endure and they don't know what an impossible task that has been thrown in teachers' laps. All they do know is that they expect every child to excel and demand high test scores that they believe reflects academic excellence.

This is America, the leader of the free world, yet today in our public schools educators are cursed, yelled at, talked back to, disobeyed, disliked and blamed. They are assaulted, harassed and their property at school is stolen and vandalized. Teachers have been shot and stabbed by students and some have been killed by students. In addition, these professional men and women are expected to motivate and educate students who are fascinated with drugs, alcohol, sex, Satanism, skinheads and gangs. They must attempt to teach the lethargic, hyperactive, rude, unresponsive and the unprepared. Add child abuse and neglect, chronic absenteeism and unreasonable parents who lie for their kids and consider teachers "the enemy" to the equation and you still only have a minuscule picture of teaching in the trenches.

The "icing on the cake" is when teachers are told it is their fault students are not learning. In the meantime, THEY are developing another "innovative program" to implement and another new teaching formula to follow that ultimately solves none of the problems.

In the middle of everything is the evaluation system for teachers—known as the "dog and pony show." Couple this with an unfair merit pay system, mounds and stacks of unnecessary paperwork and we have created a system that has not only produced a lower morale than anyone could imagine possible among educators, but also an educational system that simply does not work.

This book is not about the good students, although they are certainly mentioned. It is not about all the caring parents who make education a top priority for their children. Bless them all, for they are the ones who have kept us in the classrooms teaching the students who still want to learn. These are about the only bright spots left in teaching today.

Some may label this a "bitch book." Actually, it is a "reality book." And there are those who do not want to deal with reality and those who don't even want to hear about it. But the reality is...until parents, educators, and critics of education demand that children take responsibility for their own behavior and learning, nothing will change. **Is anyone listening...nothing will change!**

21

Until parents once again assume their responsibility of parenting, nothing will change. Schools cannot parent students or force parents to parent their own children. And believe me, they have certainly tried.

Another bright political idea will not change anything nor will another innovative teaching technique. A longer school day or a longer school year will not change it, nor will rewarding only those schools and teachers with high test scores. Test scores are not our greatest problem!

Meanwhile, we are losing experienced, unappreciated, underpaid and overworked teachers who have managed to educate millions under impossible conditions. The public has indeed received a bargain in the process.

Although there is already a tremendous shortage of certified teachers in this nation, we haven't seen anything yet! While student enrollments increase, teachers are choosing early retirement or seeking employment outside of public education. New teachers right out of college become disillusioned quickly. Reports show they leave the profession within three to five years. Nothing they learned in college prepared them for the reality of the classroom.

We are presently witnessing the last of the teachers who stayed to teach our children for ten, twenty, thirty or forty years. These are the experienced teachers who are the experts that we desperately need in our classrooms. But we have taken them for granted and we have not shown them the respect they deserve. We have not understood the magnitude of what the teaching profession has become. And certainly, we have not come close to paying them what they are worth.

Reasons for exiting the teaching field vary.....job-related stress, classroom overcrowding, disrespect from students and parents, low salaries and few benefits, and unreasonable demands from the bureaucracy.

At a recent governor's summit on education it was decided that one of our biggest problems in America is that most states don't hold teachers accountable for their students' performances. This group concluded that holding all educators accountable is the first step to reform. This notion would be laughable if it wasn't so idiotic.

I personally refuse to be held accountable for another's actions or performance over which I have no control. I will, however, be held accountable for my own actions and my own teaching performance. Nobody should expect more than that from any teacher.

Texas faced a shortage of certified teachers at the beginning of the 1996-1997 school year with 27,976 vacant teaching positions. Only 18,320 position were filled and the rest relied on *noncertified teachers* to fill these vacancies. A similar number of vacancies occurred for the 1997-1998 school year. Texas, of course, is not alone in a shortage of teachers.

Always the "innovators and trail blazers" as Texas' powers-that-be think of themselves *(regardless of the fact that Texas is 37th among the states for average teacher salaries and has a lousy retirement package)* THEY addressed the problems in education with the following brilliant ideas:

- A new teacher evaluation system that is based on whether or not a teacher is teaching his/her subject aimed directly to the latest standardized test.
- Back in 1995, our esteemed Texas Legislators established a State Board of Educator Certification to deal with our educational problems. This Board proposed that the answer lies with the quality of certified teachers in the classroom! Same song, next verse...the problem is the teacher, not the student.

Read on and see if this makes sense to you.....

Although Texas teachers now hold "lifetime certificates" these certificates would have to be renewed every five years with a renewal fee and 150 clock hours of continuing education. Failure to complete these requirements would certainly render teachers ineligible for employment as certified teachers. Forget the fact that teachers have already earned these certificates, passed all sorts of tests and climbed the now defunct career ladder. Forget too, that they have proven over and over through evaluations that they could indeed teach and that they have demonstrated their abilities time and time again in a variety of ways. I wonder what they think all the experienced teachers had been doing all those years they spent in the classroom?

The Texas legislature is notorious for changing rules in midstream *(see Chapter 8: Some People Are A Pain in the Class - Part II)*, and now it looked as if the State Board would follow suit.

There are some who believe that because this Board received a small budget with which to operate, somebody decided that charging teachers to renew their "lifetime certificates" would be a creative way to raise money. There are approximately 250,000 public school teachers in Texas. You do the math at a proposed $30 per certificate.

Now let me get this straight.....we Texans have uncertified and unqualified teachers in the classrooms because we have a shortage of qualified teachers. We are losing certified teachers by the thousands. And although Texas teachers currently attend continuing education through inservice yearly, we will solve the problems of the teacher shortage and our educational problems by sending the certified teachers back for training and selling them their own certificate every five years. I JUST DON'T GET IT. DO YOU? Does the new evaluation or the new certification address the teacher shortage or the real problems facing education? Indeed not!

As this book was nearing completion in 1998, teachers in Texas finally rose up in protest and the Board of Educator Certification was considering placing a "grandfather clause" on present certified teachers and only charging a fee to renew future teaching certificates. However, to even consider the original proposal shows the lack of common sense in the actions of those in charge of the teaching profession.

From a teacher:
"Spend one day in a classroom in America today and see what a teacher endures. I think you will be surprised, shocked and perhaps ashamed."

WHAT A FIRST YEAR TEACHER HAS TO SAY ABOUT HER FIRST SIX WEEKS OF TEACHING

"All I have ever wanted to do in my entire life was be a teacher. It has been my goal for as long as I can remember. In fact, I wanted to teach in the type of school in which I began my teaching. Our school had over 1100 sixth, seventh and eighth graders and approximately 900 of them were on free or reduced lunch. I teach reading improvement so my students were very low academically. They did not pass

the state mandated test the previous year and my job was to help them pass that year.

The best thing I can say about my first six weeks of teaching is that I did survive. Most days I went home in tears and frustration. Some days it was because I had had a rotten day and my students were totally out of control. Other days it was because I knew I couldn't help or save them all because these kids came from so many bad situations. Many didn't know who their fathers were or where they were. Others had mothers who had run away and left them or had mothers who told them they were not wanted. I had students who were on medication and others who were supposed to be on medication but refused to take it. Others bounced off the walls and should have been on some type of medication. And before it was over, I should have been on medication myself.

One of my seventh graders was already a mother. Another seventh grader was 16 years old and everyone joked that he was on the middle school five-year plan. One boy, who was even too low for special education, was stuck in my class and I was told to put him over to the side , give him easier work, and pass him on at the end of the semester.

One of my students tried to hit a teacher. I had gang leaders and those who faithfully followed their lead in class. Another student's father was suicidal and had been checked into a hospital. His mother, unable to deal with the situation, was slowly falling apart and my student literally could not function at school. He couldn't control his emotions and one day he punched a girl in the face and stomach. I had a sixth grader who ran away from home and they couldn't find him for days.

I saw in my students the results of drugs taken during pregnancy and whose brains are permanently damaged.

The first major fight in my classroom was terrifying. One child beat another one nearly to a pulp. My male aide was finally able to wrestle him to the floor and hold him down. I could go on and on...but after all, my job was to focus on preparing these kids to pass THE TEST and not to focus on problems.

Because these kids were very low academically, they had written off school. Therefore, they were extreme discipline problems and didn't care how many zeros they made. Their attitude was, "Just give me another zero, I'm not going to pass anyway."

It seemed all my time was spent on discipline and trying to teach organizational skills, of which they had none. I don't feel like I taught them much of anything. I had 17 to 20 students in each class.

I know those numbers would sound wonderful to some teachers, but with the problems these kids had and with what the school wanted me to accomplish, it was still too many. When you put that many kids with the same nature and behavior in the same class, they all feed off each other.

The end of my first six weeks as a teacher presented a grade problem. My principal was very concerned about my failure rate and how it 'looked' to others. He had me drop three zeros for everyone and told me not to give anyone a grade lower than a 65, although, I had students with averages of 9, 25, 33, etc. I did what I was told, but I did not feel it was the right thing to do. I understand the principal's point of view, but I don't agree with it. Many students were able to pass my class that six weeks who truly did not deserve it. A friend, not a teacher, told me what I did with those grades was lying. But when you are a teacher, you are told what to do and you have no say-so in the matter. Grades are changed all the time.

My principal also told me that I should stop allowing zeros and make the kids stay after school until the work is done. Should I have to have 95 of my students staying after school to finish their work everyday? It seems to me a teacher's day should end after regular classes are over. And although I am young and healthy, I am exhausted when that last bell rings every day.

I didn't give my students much homework. My department chairman said I shouldn't give homework because they don't do it anyway. My principal said I should give homework because they will give homework in high school. But when they won't do their work in class, it stands to reason they won't do their homework. These students will eventually be moved on to high school failing grades or not.

And the debate goes on. Was I prepared for teaching? I think the experiences are such that no one could really prepare for them. Until you are there, you cannot possibly know what it is like. Should I be held accountable for their performance? What do you think?"

THE ONE WEEK DIARY BY A VETERAN TEACHER ABOUT SOME OF HER "AVERAGE STUDENTS"

Charles didn't have to be dropped off at school this morning because he and his family slept in their car in the school parking lot last night. Their car has become their home.

Marie was absent again yesterday. She said her dad got drunk again and didn't get them up for school. When I asked about

26

her mother she shrugged her shoulders and said her mom was strung out on drugs and they hadn't seen her in years.

Lorena didn't do her homework again last night. She seems so tired most days but that is understandable. Mom works two jobs and Lorena has the responsibility of getting dinner and putting her younger brothers to bed at night. That seems such a big load for an eleven year old.

I talked to Albert's grandmother yesterday. She couldn't offer me any suggestions about getting him to behave in class. She said he has become uncontrollable since his mother went to prison and his dad left for California and they do not know where he is.

I kept Victoria after school today. She wants to drop out of school as soon as possible. She says since her brother was killed in a drive-by shooting she didn't care what happened to her. She believes she is doomed to the same fate.

Jennifer is sick most mornings during first period now that she is pregnant. Even though she is only thirteen she seems determined to finish school. That will mean she would graduate from high school about the same time her child begins kindergarten.

Kevin's mom was here again after school to see his teachers. She is upset that he doesn't come home from school most nights until after midnight. She wants us to help her with the problem since she is afraid he is involved with gangs. One of us already calls Kevin in the mornings to wake him up for school since mom has to be at work at 4:30 a.m. Where does our responsibility begin and end?

Rachel's mom called school today and asked if we could help with clothing for her children. Some of us pitched in and bought them shoes and we raided the school clothes closet for used clothing.

One of our teachers paid the rent for the family of one of my students. They were about to be evicted in the dead of winter.

The police confirmed today what we had suspected. Elizabeth's father has been molesting her. Thank goodness we are trained to recognize the signs and that Elizabeth trusted us enough to confide in us. Last Christmas our faculty provided Christmas, food, tree and gifts for this same family.

Jackie wasn't as lucky. She came to school with belt marks on her back, but it took the police three days to come to school and photograph the belt marks. It seems their camera had been out of film. By then, Jackie's marks had faded.

I guess those who say we don't meet the children's needs are right because I know there are many more children in my classes with needs that I know nothing about.

I prepared my lessons for next week to teach material for the standardized testing...which I do every week. After all, I have been told if the scores don't come up, they will get someone in here who can do the job. I am held accountable, you understand, and that seems to be all that is important.

Now I invite you to follow me into the "trenches" of today's schools and classrooms and get a glimpse of reality. Only the names have been changed to protect the guilty.

PUBLIC BEWARE: There is a major war going on in these trenches and there are casualties everywhere!

Chapter Three
Students: The New Breed
Teachers: The
Endangered Species

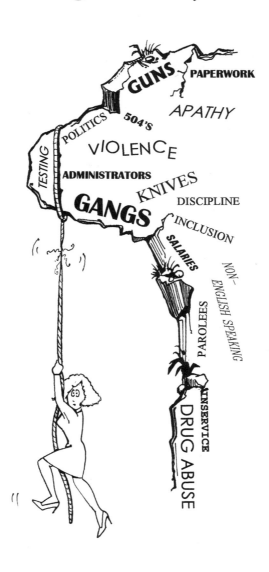

GUNS PAPERWORK

APATHY

POLITICS 504'S

TESTING VIOLENCE

ADMINISTRATORS KNIVES

GANGS DISCIPLINE

INCLUSION

SALARIES

NON-ENGLISH SPEAKING

PAROLEES

INSERVICE

DRUG ABUSE

STUDENTS: THE NEW BREED —
TEACHERS: THE ENDANGERED SPECIES

Are we raising a new breed of American children? And if we are, what will America become within the very near future? Before you decide, consider these facts taken from The Children's Defense Fund publication "The State of America's Children Yearbook 1997."

20 KEY FACTS ABOUT AMERICAN CHILDREN

1 in 2 while a preschooler has a mother in the labor force.
1 in 2 lives with a single parent at some point in childhood.
1 in 2 never complete a single year of college.
1 in 3 is born to unmarried parents.
1 in 4 is born poor.
1 in 4 is born to a mother who did not graduate from high school.
1 in 5 is born to a mother who did not receive prenatal care in the first three months of pregnancy.
1 in 5 lives in a family receiving food stamps.
1 in 5 is poor today.
1 in 6 has a foreign-born mother.
1 in 7 has no health insurance.
1 in 7 has a worker in the family but is still poor.
1 in 8 is born to a teen mother.
1 in 8 never graduates from high school.
1 in 9 is born into a family living at less than half the poverty level ($6,079 in 1995).
1 in 12 is born to a mother who received late or no prenatal care.
1 in 12 has a disability.
1 in 14 is born at a low birthrate.
1 in 21 is born to a mother who received late or no prenatal care.
1 in 25 lives with neither parent.

1 in 610 will be killed by a gun before age 20.

MOMENTS IN AMERICA FOR CHILDREN

Every 8 seconds a child drops out of school.
Every 10 seconds a child is reported abused or neglected.
Every 15 seconds a child is arrested.

Every 24 Seconds a child is born to an unmarried mother.
Every 34 seconds a child is born into poverty.
Every minute a child is born to a teen mother.
Every 2 minutes a child is born at a low birthrate.
Every 4 minutes a child is arrested for drug abuse.
Every 5 minutes a child is arrested for a violent crime.
Every 17 minutes an infant dies.
Every 92 minutes a child is killed by firearms.
Every 2 hours a child is a homicide victim.
Every 4 hours a child commits suicide.

These statistics sound like they must be from a foreign country, don't they? Nope, that is what is happening in the good old USA.

Today, teachers are faced with trying to educate the new breed of students. They are held accountable for the success or failure of every social problem that walks through their classroom doors.

Each year there are new social problems to add to the old ones. This calls for another "innovative" program to be implemented, another teaching strategy to follow, inservice on both, and then when the program is not effective and we haven't solved the problems, more new programs will be developed.

Every year we have teachers try the latest technique or program somebody dreamed up that is "all the rage." By the next year the program will be forgotten and a new one will surface that is "all the rage" for that year. And on and on it goes, year after year.

Educators are faced not only with trying to accommodate the multitude of social and behavioral problems in public schools by these constant "innovations," but there also is the serious business of preparation for THE TEST. In addition, there are vast amounts of paper work and the everyday problems teachers face just trying to teach their classes. Teachers are left wringing their hands with frustration, bewilderment and anger. They are abandoning ship because teaching has become such a calamity.

Inner city schools have more serious problems than urban schools. And urban schools have more problems than rural schools. Affluent schools have different problems from non-affluent schools. However, teachers in any community in any state will tell you that this new breed of student behavior is sometimes appalling with attitudes often horrendous.

Everyone knows the family structure is no longer the support system it once was. Coupled with this and the increasing interference of a bureaucracy that issues unrealistic mandates, teachers are left on their own with an impossible job.

To determine the real problems and some realistic solutions, we do not need another state or federal study, or another national research program or survey. We do not need another education commission or in-depth report. We need only to ask the teachers in America: where the problems are, which solutions will work and which will not, and what might keep them in the classroom. And the answers will not cost taxpayers millions of dollars in fees or take years to complete.

A school, after all, is not a General Motors assembly line where the parts are standard and can be designed, molded, constructed and mass produced into one final product. Realistically, the parts are all different and some are substandard. And these parts will never be molded and mass produced into one successful product.

Here are some teacher's thoughts on the subject:

"I am tired of reading and hearing the theme, teachers can't teach. Why can't people understand that many students cannot or will not learn because of factors outside the teacher's control?" Veronica I.

"How can I be held responsible for what I have no control over?" Michelle F.

"Teachers are not medical professionals, but we can tell you that many of our students are the product of the drug culture in which their parents participated. Not only do we see the slow students, we see the blank eyes looking back at us." Crystal B.

"Most American students are in school just to get by. They have not been taught the value of learning at home." Tom L.

"There are many good students who can read, write, do math and think for themselves. They take pride in their work and look to the future. These are the ones who have kept us in the classroom up until now." Rachel R.

"We still teach happy, well-adjusted kids who come to school and learn. They are not, however, in the majority." Charlotte V.

"I see tomorrow's citizens who will run this country and it scares me to death. It would scare everybody else if they could see what I see every day." Carrie B.

Students today lack the very basics in manners and social skills. Kids find nothing wrong with combing their hair at the lunch table, throwing food, kissing and embracing in public and loudly belching or worse in class. They curse like sailors and talk and boo during public functions. Addressing adults with "yes sir" and "no sir" and "yes ma'am" and "no ma'am" is rare today. Good manners and common courtesy seem to be a thing of the past for most of the younger generation.

Reports of child neglect, abuse and incest are increasing. The children on the receiving end of these despicable abuses are found in classrooms across America. These kids are depressed, angry, defeated, distrusting and rebellious. And who can blame them?

Straight from the trenches are these teacher observations:

"Students display rude behavior and they do not really realize they are rude. They have never been taught what is rude." David J.

"The deprived state of the children in my school is shocking. We have a terrible problem with head lice and body filth. The kids arrive at school not fed and go home to empty houses. They are virtually raising themselves." Ann C.

"One summer I worked for the YMCA of Dallas. Our purpose was to get the younger kids of the ghettos off the streets and into creative teaching programs. I will never forget a field trip we took to a Dallas area lake and one youngster who ran to the edge of Lake Grapevine, looked across the water and called excitedly, 'Look! Oh look, there's Europe!' He had never been more than ten blocks away from home." Georgia S.

"Children these days are allowed to choose everything for themselves. They often decide when they will go to bed, when or if they will get up and go to school and how well they will behave and learn if they do attend school." Brian Q.

"Today's children have less respect for themselves, their work,

their teachers and school. Even their attitude toward each other is hostile and uncaring." Darlene L.

"I see more and more kids desperately looking for someone to admire and believe in. There are so many emotionally starved kids who would rather have negative attention than to have no attention. When you have two or three kids in a class with this problem, teachers can't win. Our time is spent trying to control disruption after disruption." Rose R.

"Parents are overworked, uneducated and living in a world that they believe offers little hope for change. Their desperation and insecurities are projected through their children. Does this make for supportive parents? Of course not. And the scenario will be repeated when these kids have kids." Mark M.

"I am so afraid that a solid and secure family life is becoming a thing of the past. If that is the case, this nation might just as well throw in the towel now, because schools cannot provide an alternative or an answer to the problem." Sandra O.

"I taught a young lady in junior high who once spit in my face. She is grown now and I saw her recently. She was glad to see me and remembered the good things I had tried to do for her. I doubt she remembered she had spit in my face, or ever understood how wrong it was." Michelle H.

"My colleagues and I have been told by junior high students to 'shut-up' and 'get your f—ing hands off me.' If the public thinks this doesn't happen very often in classrooms, they are dead wrong. The f word and the b word are used quite frequently among students." Kay E.

"Discipline today is more and more paperwork. There are too many rules and steps to follow to ensure there are no legal fights. We have to be careful about discrimination accusations, what is said, how the parents will react and will the administration back us. What a nightmare!" Jane A.

"Teachers take verbal abuse because students get by with it at home as well as at school. There is really nothing a student won't say to a teacher these days." Erica J.

"There is too much frustration for teachers and administrators. You are not encouraged to take a stand about anything because you must 'cover your ass.' Teachers are told to call the parents when kids misbehave. Administrators don't want to handle the problem. If you call long enough, you may finally get a parent at home who either doesn't want to be bothered, or who takes the kid's side, or who doesn't speak English. And while we are trying to call a parent what do they expect us to do with a classroom full of students? That's our problem!" James B.

"Teachers should not have to put up with disruptive student behavior and that's the bottom line. These students should lose the right to a free public education without any apologies from us." Erin M.

"The new catch phrase now in some states is Zero Tolerance in the classroom. That is suppose to mean that teachers do not have to continue to be tolerant of misbehavior. It sounds great, but there are too many loopholes for it to be effective. Time will tell just how tolerant or intolerant the administration will to be. So far, I haven't seen any difference." Jacque R.

"Principals who are not backed by central administration do not back teachers. When central administration is not backed by the school board because of the fear of law suits, you can see where the buck stops...with the teacher, of course." Mary L.

"We had one junior high student who kicked another student, broke his nose and knocked out three teeth. The police arrested him, but he was back in school the following day. What clear message do you think that sent to both students and teachers?" Wayne B.

"One of our students raped his sister and set her on fire. He continued to attend school even though he was emotionally disturbed. He was mainstreamed into the middle of regular junior high classes. His favorite pastime was rubbing up against teachers and female students at every opportunity." Larry H.

"A young man at our school pushed a vice-principal up against the wall with a chair and only missed a half day of school. Teachers and administrators have been both physically and verbally assaulted by students because we allow this behavior in our schools." Mary M.

"I had a student tell me, 'You just might wake up and find your-self in a hospital tomorrow.' Nothing was done to the student because he was 'emotionally disturbed'." Jack I.

Police officers arrest kids in the act of vandalizing, stealing or assaulting. The law protects the kids by releasing them to their parents who send them back into the schools. Fourteen and fifteen year old kids curse and spit at police officers and little is done because they are juveniles. Gangs deface buildings and schools. Weapons, drugs and alcohol are confiscated in schools every day. It is not unusual anymore to see kids hand-cuffed and removed from school for some offense...only to return to school the next day. There is no shame connected with being arrested among young people. To them, this is no big deal.

Despite trying to educate young people about the dangers of drugs, the sale of drugs and rehabilitation facilities is thriving.

According to experts, drug problems are starting earlier and earlier — at 11 and 12 years of age. Alcohol comes first, marijuana is second and there seems to be a tie between cocaine, heroin and LSD as drug use progresses. There are a lot of drugs out there and they are a lot more potent than in times past.

Flight by families to small towns or to the suburbs has not been an answer for drug protection. Some kids are "hooked" after their first drug experience while others simply do drugs because it "feels good" or because of personal problems. And what about the danger factor? They have the fallacy that nothing is going to happen to them.

I shall never forget the young man who asked how much money I made in a month teaching school after we had a class discussion on the importance of an education and the ability to earn a living. After giving him a ballpark figure of the amount, he replied, "I can make more than that in less than a week selling drugs! Why should I get an education?" The fact that it was against the law and there was the threat of prison time or worse made no impression on him.

When names of juveniles are not published as their crimes make the press, this continues to send a clear message that while they are breaking the law, we will protect them.

Kids attending public schools all over America are on probation for felony crimes. They are sitting next to students who

36

would never dream of breaking the law. They brag to their friends about what they have done and how they got away with it. The time is fast approaching when schools will need their own fully staffed police force if there isn't a drastic change in the behavior of the children in our society. Not one or two police officers, as many schools presently have, but a police force.

THE NEW BREED AND THE LAW

The time is long overdue when we stop allowing juveniles to freely break the law. They must be made to realize that if they are willing to commit a crime, they must suffer the consequences. Fear of breaking the law doesn't concern many American young people. We cannot change the families of our young people, but we can change how we deal with the actions of these kids...both in public schools and on the streets.

Juveniles are being charged with murder at an alarming rate. Not only are they killing their parents, their grandparents and each other, teens are killing for expensive car wheels, jackets, shoes or just for the thrill of it. Gangs are killing each other and innocent bystanders. They are heaping havoc on society. Everybody is aware of this. Yet, we sit back and allow it to continue.

This new breed of young people who have no respect for the law or respect for human life becomes the adults who are walking our streets or filling our prison systems to overflowing. Then, after release from prison they return to the streets again to control our lives.

The new breed of students are being nurtured at home, in public schools and in the community with the help of our tolerance, apathy, outdated laws and refusal as a society to demand that legislators make changes in the laws, and judges to uphold these laws. Control must be given back to law-abiding citizens. Until we become the direct victims of a crime ourselves, it seems to be easier to do nothing and just let criminals and the bureaucracy continue to run our lives.

What kind up wake-up call do we need? When children are breaking the law and committing murder, isn't this enough? What can be said about a country that cannot even control their young people?

The following deliberate acts of homicide and mayhem scare the hell out of me:

37

- In Chicago, two pre-teens dropped a five year old out a high rise window. Also in Chicago, three grade-schoolers broke into a home and beat an infant to death.

- A band member was shot and killed at a football game by a gang member from another school.

- A star football player was shot and killed by a female student while he was standing in the high school cafeteria line waiting to eat breakfast. In other schools in the same area, there were two beatings, one attempted murder, one rape and two murders.

- A student was shot and killed inside a high school in Irving, Texas, in the middle of change of classes as more than a thousand students were walking around. Also in Irving, gang members randomly shot a gun in the food court of a mall, killing a man who was eating with his wife and child.

- In Fort Worth, a young teacher was stabbed to death as she entered her portable classroom to prepare for the opening of school.

- Elsewhere, three teenage shoplifters shot to death an innocent bystander at a mall after he had joined in the pursuit to apprehend them. He had been married only a week.

- Five teenagers invited a small audience to watch as they ambushed and killed a food delivery man for $18 worth of food. The teenagers ranged in age from 13 to 18 years old.

- In Dallas, several outstanding high school football players ran a theft ring when they were not in school or playing football.

- In October, 1997 in Pearl, Miss., a 16-year old was accused of killing his mother and then going to school and shooting nine students. Two of them died. Accused along with him of conspiracy are six friends believed to be a group practicing Satanism.

- In December, 1997, in Kentucky, a 14-year old fired a gun in the hallway of a high school killing three students and wounding five more.

- In 1997, in Arkansas, a 14-year old boy shot and wounded two students.

- In Oregon, in 1998, a freshman was charged with killing his parents at home and then walking into school and killing two students.

- In Dallas, in 1998, three boys ages 7, 8 and 11 were taken into police custody for allegedly kidnapping and sexually assaulting a 3-year old girl. According to police, the little girl was lured away from her yard, clubbed with a brick and a shoe, stripped, sexually assaulted and dragged to a creek where she was left. The little girl survived the attack, but who could imagine such a crime taking place in this country? The 7 and 8-year olds cannot be prosecuted because they are under the age of 10. The 11 year old faces charges up to 40 years, first in a juvenile facility and then prison.

- And who will ever forget the 11-year old and 13-year old accused of killing four students and a teacher and wounding ten others in Jonesboro, Arkansas, also in 1998?

- As this book goes to press, our country is still in shock and disbelief at the massacre that happened at Columbine High School in Colorado.

What could cause such rage in a young person that they would commit such unspeakable crimes?

Although all the violence in public schools shocked citizens in this country, it did not shock some teachers.

What *does* shock teachers is when there has been no violence in their school by the end of a school year. You cannot experience anger, intimidation, aggressive behavior and hostile attitudes without knowing you are sitting on a powder keg. And for the quiet student who is a loner and "something is just not quite right," the same applies.

What do we expect? There is very little limit put on kids today and their behavior. When students believe rules are to be broken and don't apply to them...rules will be broken. When there is no respect for authority —either at home, at school or on the streets — then there is no power in authority. And when families are dysfunctional, kids are dysfunctional.

The sole purpose in writing this book was to say to the public: Listen! This country has a big problem with our kids! It isn't like it use to be. The little red school house with the scrubbed and starched eager little children is gone. In its place we have a battle zone. Teachers are afraid for themselves and for their students.

Although crimes happen in schools every day, we seldom hear about them. Most crimes don't make the local or national news. Perhaps, they should.

While faculty members are at school their cars are stolen and stripped, tires slashed, hood ornaments removed, windows and side mirrors smashed and paint scraped off with sharp instruments.

There have been numerous drive-by shootings by gang members around schools and students are terrorized and threatened by gangs. Lunch money is stolen or taken from students and money and credit cards are stolen from teachers' purses. These may not be the crimes of the century, but they are important to those on the receiving end. And if nothing else, schools should be safe places for every student and every teacher.

What do teachers have to say on the subject of the new breed? Read on...

"Lying, cheating and stealing seems to have become a way of life. When students are caught, few seem to be ashamed, embarrassed or remorseful." Lane W.

"Our society had better start caring and do something about the fact that students have a complete lack of respect for themselves, each other, school authority and the law." Barton M.

"We cannot undo what has been done at home with these kids and their appalling morals. But we shouldn't have to put up with them and their criminal behavior. When will this country again give a damn about our rights?" Bess M.

"I read that child support caseworkers voted this father's excuse for not paying child support as one of the worst excuses they had heard: 'I can't afford to pay child support. I have to pay my cable TV bill.' This is a perfect example of parenting in our country today. And just what type of parents will their kids make?" Jacob W.

"So many children today are 'older' than their ages. They should get to be children before they are adults. Some children, born addicted to crack and heaven knows what else, deserve specialized care and training. But teachers are suppose to pull another rabbit out of the hat and take responsibility for their learning and raise those damn test scores!" Barbara P.

"There is no way I can teach everything I'm suppose to teach, and in addition, teach many things kids should have learned at home. I am organized in every aspect of teaching. I am also single, therefore, I have no family obligations. However, I can barely keep my head above water because the pressures in school overwhelm me. I have no idea how a teacher can teach and manage a family, too." Grace T.

"I was hired to teach, but I am given little opportunity to do so. I cannot work learning miracles if I have to fight all the outside influences. I cannot be responsible for my student's actions or their parents actions. I can only be responsible for my own actions." Gail I.

"There is the increasing removal of freedom to be creative, inventive and imaginative in teaching today. There is too much testing and preparing for testing, documentation of everything imaginable and fighting the daily battles in the classroom. It is time for me to move on." Lisa L.

"We see increasing numbers of disturbed children and low IQs in our classrooms, but we are still expected to 'RAISE THOSE TEST SCORES'." Janet H.

"The majority of students today have the attitude, 'I don't care and you can't make me.' Teachers care, but they have become absolutely overwhelmed with it all. I wish classrooms across America could be secretly videotaped and played on national television. The public would be in for quite a shock!" Helen S.

"I was asked if I was ever afraid at school. Of course I am. There are dangerous and crazy kids at school. And not just one or two, but many. Don't think for a minute there aren't crazy and dangerous parents also in the mix. Teaching is like sitting on top of a volcano...an active volcano." Jan M.

The new breed and the endangered species who are held accountable for their education are on a collision course. And if our teachers possess such magical powers that they can fulfill all that is expected of them — under almost impossible circumstances — they are less respected and appreciated and more grossly underpaid than we thought. When these teachers are gone, who will replace them?

An employment advertisement for teachers should read something like this:

WANTED: PUBLIC SCHOOL TEACHERS

QUALIFICATIONS: MUST HAVE A MINIMUM OF ONE COLLEGE DEGREE AND CERTIFICATION BY THE STATE.

IN ADDITION TO TEACHING DUTIES, MUST BE WILLING AND ABLE TO BE ALL OF THE FOLLOWING: BOOKKEEPER, RECORDKEEPER, ENTERTAINER, HUMORIST, LECTURER, GUARD, NURSE, JANITOR, POLICEMAN/POLICEWOMAN, NEGOTIATOR, PEACEMAKER, COUNSELOR, POLITICIAN, PLAYMATE, TUTOR, ORGANIZER, IDEA MAKER, MOTIVATOR, LEADER, DIPLOMAT, SURROGATE PARENT AND SCAPEGOAT.

MUST BEGIN WORK IN AUGUST. SALARY SCHEDULE NOT AVAILABLE UNTIL MID SEPTEMBER. PAID ONCE PER MONTH.

SALARIES DECREASE WITH EXPERIENCE IN COMPARISON TO BEGINNING SALARIES.   AFTER HOURS WORK REQUIRED WITH NO OVERTIME PAY.

RETIREMENT BENEFITS ARE MINIMAL IN COMPARISON TO OTHER PROFESSIONS.

APPLICANT MUST HAVE THE PATIENCE OF JOB, THE ENDURANCE OF A CAMEL, THE STRENGTH OF A BULL AND THE COURAGE OF A SWAT TEAM.

Chapter Four
Dear Teacher

DEAR TEACHER

Every day of the week teachers receive notes from parents regarding their child's absence from school. Often, these notes bring smiles, laughter and sometimes total dismay. After reading some of these excuses, teachers still haven't the vaguest idea why the student was absent. The following is a collection of actual notes, from actual parents with actual spelling intact. Only the names have been changed to protect everybody.

Physical education classes probably wins the prize for the most notable notes:

DEAR TEACHER...

- Please don't let Molly spread her legs in P.E.

- Please excuse Jane from P. E. She has a sore foot. She heard it last night.

- Betty Sue was absent because she was in bed with gramps.

- Peter was absent because he hurt his growing playing football.

- Please excuse Brenda from any activitys today. She feel last night and bend her foot back, spranged her Big toe, swallow and very sore.

- Please excuse sue from Jim. She has a sore foot.

- Joe had not went to school because his Grandfather had past a way. And I could not take him and bring him. Because his grandmother lives fare.

- Something is bitting Jill's legs and arms when she is in P.E. I don't no what it is but it makes nots on her.

- Please excuse Margie from P.E. today. She stopped on a nail and has hunt her foot.

- Excuse Barbara June from P.E. She feel off a tree and misplaced her hip.

- Excuse Toni from jim. She is administrating.

- My son is under a doctor's care and should not take any fizical education.

- Excuse Bubba from P.E. He has very loose vowels.

- Excuse Jenny. She is having problems with her ovals.

- Excuse Darla for not going to school but she had to see her ant that died.

- Reed has been sick with the various.

- Please excuse james. He had a stomach.

- Please excuse Randal from P.E. He heard his back yesterday.

- Judy has a crute in her neck. Edcuite her from P.E.

- Please excuse Allison from P.E. because she got bit buy a dog hard, and she's got a fraktured elbow.

- Please excuse John from being absent. He's been very sick with stomach craps.

- Oscar had a bad pain on his side and doctor said they were caused by gases.

- Please excuse Eddie. He injured his fart.

- Eric was absent because of the flew.

THIS NOTE WAS EVERYBODY'S FAVORITE

Please don't let Sandra have P.E. because
she is on her . wright now.

(After much discussion, the conclusion was reached that Sandra couldn't be on her dot, so she must be on her period!)

47

AND THESE STUDENTS HAD TERRIBLE PROBLEMS

- Would it be possible for Jimmy to be taken out of P.E. He has a personal problem which makes him not want to take it. He has been in the hospital for delayed puberty and he still hasn't started yet.

- Please excuse Dick from being absent. He had deahrea *(crossed out)* diaarea *(crossed out)* dyrea *(crossed out)* the shits.

- Billy has been out of school with the shits.

- Deana has seazzers and she takes medicine for them. If she is fixing to have one she will turn white and get dizze. Give her an extra table. Also she is not to be wiped at school. She can't be upset because she has a heart mermur and can't have too much salt.

- Evelyn was absent because she had a fever, sore throat, head-ache, and upset stomach. Her sister was sick too with fever and sore throat, her brother had a fever. There must be the flu going around. Her father even got hot last night.

TEACHERS ARE ALWAYS AMAZED WHEN PARENTS THINK THEIR KID IS THE ONLY ONE IN SCHOOL AND ALL THEIR INDI-VIDUAL NEEDS SHOULD BE MET...

- Jane would rather wear her own shorts than a baggy gym suit and I quite agree with her. Of course, if you would like to purchase a suit for her and have it altered to fit her properly, feel free to do so.

- May doesn't like P.E. and especially when she doesn't know anyone in class. She would like to have her fourth and fifth periods changed around. She knows a girl fourth period.

THE SPELLING AND SENTENCE STRUCTURE IN THESE NOTES OPENS UP A WHOLE NEW WORLD...

- Will you please start serving breakfast a little earyler so people who go to tootering can get there on time?

- I don't understand about all this detention. I think it is unfare. When I wads a student their was no such thing.

- Janette was absent on 10/9 for know reason.

- Malcom didn't go to school because he didn' want to.

- Becky was absent from school for she has a kenney infection.

- Ed was absent because he had a cruick in his nect and he can't turn his heard. *(Everybody should be able to turn their heard!)*

- Lisa was late because her alarm failed.

- Darren was ill yesterday and couldn't come.

- Please excuse Carol Monday. Her arm and fingers were swole.

- Becky was absent because she was ill of her foot.

- Sue was absent because she was sick at her stomach and voting.

- Excuse David. He had a lot of bomit and couldn't go.

- Tony's let was sore and did not fell good.

- My daughter did not went to school because she had the momps.

- Skuse Laura of being absent. She had a lot of feaver and had a bad caught.

- My daughter must stay off her foat as much as possible and apple ice pack twice a day untilll better. *(Say what?)*

- Please excuse June on Monday. She was raped on Sunday.

- Excuse Johnny. He misted the bus.

- Lane was absent from school. He got sick. He gets well today.

- Joe was absent from school yesterday because he was in a bad mood. *(Why can't that work for teachers, too!)*

- Monroe was absent because his dog had puppies.

THIS NOTE TO A TEACHER WINS THE SWEEPSTAKES!

Dear Mrs. Jones,
I don't know what's wrong with you. You expect the kids to learn something new every week.

Chapter Five
Dear Parent

AND THIS JUST IN . . .
TEENAGE CRIME IS UP,
TEST SCORES ARE DOWN,
. . . TEACHERS ARE HELD
ACCOUNTABLE.

DEAR PARENT

I WISH I HAD A DOLLAR FOR EVERY TIME I HEARD...

"Can I have a Kleenex?"

"Can I sharpen my pencil?"

"Can I go to the restroom?"

"Can I get a drink of water?"

"Can I go to the nurse?"

"Can I go to my locker?"

"Can I borrow a pencil?"

"Can I borrow some paper?"

"Can I borrow a book?"

***

"I didn't do my homework. I forgot."

"I left my homework in my mother's car."

"My little brother ate my homework."

"My mother washed my homework in my jeans."

"I didn't have time to study for the test."

"I hate to read."

"Do we *have* to write that down?"

"I'm not in the mood to dress-out for P.E."

"Why do we have to learn *that*?"

***

"I didn't hear you."

"I don't have any paper."

***

"I didn't understand that."

"I wasn't listening."

"I wasn't talking."

"I didn't know we were having a test."

"How many questions on the test?"

"What's the date?"

"What time does the bell ring?"

"Are we going to do anything today?"

"What are we going to do today?"

"Did we do anything while I was absent?"

***

"I forgot what you told us to do."

"I don't feel like doing anything today."

"I feel like I'm going to throw uppppp....

ohhh, I'm sorry, I got it on your shoes!"

***

"I'm in a bad mood!"

"I wasn't looking out the window."

"I wasn't talking, Joe was."

"Why do you always think I'm talking?"

"This is boring."

"I hate school."

"How can I look it up in the dictionary if I can't spell it?"

"I'm tired and I have to work after school."

"I'm tired because I watched TV until 2:00 in the morning."

"I have more important things to do than homework."

"I wasn't sleeping, I was just resting my eyes."

"You expect too much."

"I've got too many problems to worry about school."

"I'm late because I couldn't get my locker open."

"Huh?"

"I *hate* to read!"

"I don't care! **Just gimme a zero!**"

Chapter Six
Inclusion And Confusion

"WE'RE LOOKING FOR A FEW GOOD MEN AND WOMEN

...WITH LARGE BLADDERS!"

INCLUSION AND CONFUSION

It's Monday morning and time to begin another week of grueling combat at Everywhere Middle School. As you walk into the halls of the school building, students will come at you from all directions...some seemingly at 90 miles per hour. You learn very quickly to dodge, side-step and crouch just to stay in one piece. The movement becomes an acquired skill.

You will hear language that would make the toughest adult gasp. It makes no difference whether you are in elementary, middle school, or high school — four-letter words and curse words are a large part of the vocabulary of today's children.

The school police officer nods hello as he heads for his office on the first floor. Dressed in uniform *(complete with bullet-proof vest under his shirt)*, shoulder radio, mace, nightstick and service revolver, he is in attendance eight hours a day, five days a week, during the school year. Male teachers with no special equipment and female teachers, dressed only in bras of their choice underneath their clothing *(non bullet-proof ones at that)* have no radio, no mace, no nightstick and no weapon.

The ladies hurry to their classrooms to lock up their purses for the day. On the way, they observe obscene printing on student clothing, shaved heads and partially shaved heads. Boys are wearing earrings and ponytails or messages shaved on their heads, while others have two-toned hair color. Girls are decked out in shorts and black pantyhose with large torn holes and army boots on their feet. They are all trying to make fashion statements, but nobody has a clue what that statement might be.

Mrs. Sally Porter unlocks her classroom door, locks her purse in a drawer of the filing cabinet, hangs the keys around her neck and gets ready for her first period class. Mrs. Porter teaches eighth graders computer literacy. There are 30 computers in her classroom, three of which are not in working order. She has 28 students with only 27 working computers, but this will not be a problem. It is rare when all of her students are present at the same time.

First Period

As she calls roll, Mrs. Porter looks around the room and mentally evaluates her students...as she does every day. Five are non-English speaking students. Two of those understand no

English at all and the other three understand only a few words. Mrs. Porter does not speak Spanish or Vietnamese. Four students are deaf and are accompanied by an interpreter who will "sign".

Eight others are "at risk" students and all of these have special modifications that must be followed in instruction, grading and behavior. Modifications are different for each of the eight.

Six others are special education students who have varied learning disabilities and special modifications must be followed for each of them. Modifications are different for each of these six.

Four of the remaining students are average to above average academically, do not exhibit behavior problems and receive no special directives.

Student number 28 is repeating the eighth grade and also repeated the seventh grade. He is on parole for gang activity and breaking and entering. He has no intention of learning nor is he cooperative. He is in school only because a judge and his parole officer demands it. Today he is absent. Mrs. Porter is glad.

Four of her students were absent on Friday. She must write four admission forms for their other classes. One student has no note from her parent, so Mrs. Porter writes her an unexcused absence. The student will still be allowed to make up the work she missed with the unexcused absence. Students are absent so often that if zeros were given for all unexcused absences, few would pass. Two students were out with "pink eye" and Mrs. Porter hopes she doesn't get it, too. The other student stayed at home to baby-sit her siblings while her mother was at the hospital giving birth to her seventh child. Three football players have brought athletic forms to be completed by all their teachers to reflect the player's academic and conduct grades. Mrs. Porter must average their grades before the end of class.

Mrs. Porter re-teaches the material she taught the previous Friday. Some of those who were in attendance on Friday act as if they never heard the information and cannot answer any questions on the subject.

The door opens and a new student walks into the room. Mrs. Porter must now take time to assign him a seat, give him a copy of the class rules and a supply list. She must also find out how much the student does and does not know about the subject matter she has covered in her class for the past twelve weeks.

She discovers that the student has moved many times during the semester. He cannot type and knows very little about the operation of the computer. She will have to go back to square one with this student and provide him with a great deal of individualized instruction. Now, Mrs. Porter has 29 students in her first period class.

In her school, there are eight periods in the typical school day. Seven periods are 45 minutes each with five minutes between classes. There is a 90 minute lunch period to accommodate all students, with 30 minutes for lunch for each class.

Mrs. Porter begins the day's new lesson which is paragraph indention using the TAB key and an oral review of spacing rules for sentence punctuation. The assignment is to type two short paragraphs with proper indention, correct spacing and to proofread carefully before printing the paragraphs. She must enlist the help of students who are fluent in both English and Spanish to explain the assignment to the Spanish-non-English-speaking students. She must show the Asian students what she wants them to do the best way she can. There are no Asian speaking tutors in the room. Do they understand? She does not know. Time will tell.

Three "at risk" students did not bother to listen to either the review, the lesson or the assignment. One of these students is busy removing the tops of keys and switching them around on the computer while the other two are having a conversation about their week-end at a party where beer was served. Mrs. Porter can repeat the entire lesson and assignment for them but she doesn't have time. She must help the non-English speaking students who are trying very hard to complete their assignment. If the three who didn't listen do not complete the assignment they will receive zeros. They don't care.

Two special education students who are very low academically must be shown individually (two times) what to do before they understand the lesson.

Albert who disrupts class at least once every day has just called the student sitting next to him "a damn fag." This is not appropriate behavior so Mrs. Porter must stop what she is doing, write a referral form to the office and send the student on his way. Before he leaves the room he gives her his best "go to hell" look.

The office sends Albert back to class with this notation:
Albert was given a warning. Call his parents. **Result:** Mrs. Porter cannot stop her class and call his parents and what could Mom or Pop do about the situation now, anyway? **Bottom line:** The office didn't want to deal with Albert. Mrs. Porter is frustrated, but Albert is happy as a lark. A call to the parents that evening may or may not help the situation in the future. The Alberts of the classroom thrive on constant disruptions.

An office aide enters the room with passes for two students to report to the school nurse for eye testing. All eyes are now on the departing students and the assignment is   forgotten for the moment.

Student number 28 *(B. J. the parolee)* arrives in class late. He has missed more than half of the class, but this is not unusual. He is part of a growing number of students who cannot or will not get to school on time. B. J. makes a big production of getting to his seat and all eyes are now focused on him. With less than fifteen minutes left in the class period, he will learn nothing today. However, he has repeatedly told Mrs. Porter that he is here only because he has to be and to just give him zeros.

As the bell rings to end the period, Mrs. Porter has devoted little or no attention to the average or above average students. There was no time. Mrs. Porter has six more classes to teach. Perhaps, she can still feel a sense of accomplishment sometime today.

Between first and second periods, Mrs. Porter had high hopes of racing to the restroom. Instead, she must average the football player's grades and then write three late passes for their next classes.

If a study has not already been made, The National Institute of Health should certainly conduct a serious review on the stamina of teacher's bladders. Those with the largest bladders are the lucky ones. Those with average size and small size bladders are to be commended.

It is a well known fact that no school in America has an adequate amount of faculty restrooms. This is because given the amount of time allotted teachers for this particular bodily function during the school day, they are expected to "go" before they get to school. Between classes, teachers are generally expected to monitor the halls and check student restrooms for vandals, fighters, smokers and dopers. If nature persists, you can usually find a line of teachers in front of the faculty restroom during a change of classes...waiting patiently, standing on one foot and then the other while silently praying they will get their turn before the bell rings.

Teachers are not encouraged to leave their classrooms unattended for anything as mundane as a restroom visit. Should nature be unkind enough to inappropriately call and a teacher must leave class, this will probably be when: Stevie knocks Bubba out of his seat, or a student will have a seizure, or an emotionally disturbed student will decide it is time to beat the hell out of another student because "he looked at me." Girls are fighters these days, too. Some females are actually rougher and tougher than the males. In fact, some of our young "ladies" could hold their own with sumo-wrestlers.

Leaving a class unattended is when Sally June would decide this is the opportune time to tie into Effie Mae with both fists, because "she talked to my boyfriend."

Mrs. Porter will never forget the eighth grade girl who brought a loaded gun to class and kept it in a paper sack at her desk for two days debating whether or not to shoot her boyfriend. Fortunately, she decided against it, but Mrs. Porter was terrified that she was not aware of the drama until it was over.

It hasn't been too long ago that Mrs. Porter had another brush with a student "packing heat." Tony was a hyperactive special education student who disrupted class every chance he got and drove all of his teachers crazy. No matter how hard they tried, there was little that was likable about this kid. No type of punishment improved his behavior. Nothing seemed to phase him.

Finally, the day came when Mrs. Porter had had more than enough of Tony. After one disruption then another, she put him in the hall outside her classroom with his book bag and told him to keep his mouth closed until the bell rang. A few minutes later as she was busy teaching, Tony crawled back into the classroom, dragging his large book bag behind him, disrupting the class once again. Mrs. Porter, now completely void of patience for Tedious Tony, grabbed him by the arm and escorted him into the hall. She tossed his book bag behind him and verbally let her temper fly, eyes blazing.

Two hours later, while Mrs. Porter was attempting to gulp down her lunch in the 25 minutes allowed her, she was informed by the principal that Tedious Tony had been toting **two loaded handguns** in his infamous book bag. Although all of his teachers — as well as the administration — knew this student was seriously disturbed, he was perfectly capable of using those guns if the right buttons were pushed. Why was he still allowed to attend a public school? Because it is the law that no student can be denied a public education...unless, of course, he/she should kill someone.

Mrs. Porter...to be continued.

THE TRANSITION OF INCLUSION

What is inclusion? The Individuals with Disabilities Education Act, originally enacted as the Education for All Handicapped Children Act, was created by Congress to assist states in providing children with disabilities with a free appropriate public education. A requirement of an "appropriate" public education is that each child with a disability be educated in the "least restrictive environment." States are required to provide procedures to ensure that children with disabilities are educated "to the maximum extent appropriate" <u>with non-disabled children in regular classes.</u>

Mainstreaming refers to the part-time placement of students with disabilities in regular classrooms. Inclusion refers to the merging of special and regular education so that students with disabilities receive special education and regular education support while they are full-time members of the regular classroom. The leaders of inclusion use the rationale that led to desegregation for black students as the standard that is moving the dual system of special and regular education toward a completely integrated system. That rationale is:

"Segregation is the way in which society tells a group of human beings that they are inferior to other groups of human beings in that society." *(Testimony by Kenneth Clark in Brown vs. The Board of Education-1956)*

Inclusion simply means:

- All children learn together in the same classroom with the necessary services and supports to be successful.
- Children with disabilities are educated in regular age-appropriate classrooms and schools.
- Children are educated with non-disabled peers, regardless of the severity of the disability.

61

- All children attend their home school; the school they would attend if they did not have a disability.
- All children participate in all aspects of school.
- Children with and without disabilities have opportunities to interact and develop friendships with one another.
- Teachers work in cooperative and collaborative teams that include regular and special educators (including related service professionals).
- Emphasis is placed on abilities and possibilities.
- The program is designed according to the educational needs of individual students.

WHO IS INVOLVED IN INCLUSION?

Special education includes these students: ADHD (Attention Deficit, Hyperactivity Disorder), ADD (Attention Deficit Disorders), ED (Emotionally Disturbed), LD (Leaning Disabled), Visually Impaired/Blind, Hearing Impaired/Deaf, Orthopedically Handicapped, Autistic, Speech or Language Impaired, Mentally Retarded, Multi-Handicapped, and Traumatic Brain Injured.

Other students may be classified as Code 504 which includes a much broader list than special education. However, all students who qualify for special education also qualify under Code 504.

Who is eligible under Section 504? Any student who has a physical or mental impairment that substantially limits a major life activity such as: walking, seeing, hearing, caring for oneself, performing manual tasks, breathing, learning, speaking, or working. Each of these categories defines specific handicaps from obesity to allergies and social maladjustments to conduct disorders. "At Risk" or potential dropout students are also included.

Because the list is so broad, it would be simpler to list conditions which are *not* covered by Code 504. These would include: homosexuality and bisexuality, transvestitism, pedophilla, exhibitionism, voyeurism, physical impairments or other sexual behavior disorders, compulsive gambling, kleptomania, pyromania and the use or possession of illegal drugs or alcohol.

Do not, however, be surprised if these conditions are later added to the list. Is there anyone out there who understands why there might be some difficulty in trying to teach in the classrooms of this nation's public schools?

The hearts of teachers go out to any child who is handicapped in any form or fashion. Their hearts also go out to the parents of these children. Do these children belong in regular classrooms in public schools? The collective minds of the brightest educators in the world do not know for sure if the answer to that question is yes or no. Are we doing these children an injustice putting them in the mainstream of public schools or are we doing them an injustice if they are kept out of the mainstream?

One thing is very clear and that is the injustice done to the regular classroom teacher who is not trained to teach these special education students. Also, the negative impact this has on the students who are not special education students is pronounced. In a fair and perfect world, the ideal answer would be to have special education teachers accompany these students into the mainstream of regular classrooms and teach with the regular teacher. However, this is not a fair or perfect world, and the bureaucracy would never put that much money into public education. It is much easier for the bureaucracy to continue adding to an already thankless, low paying, difficult and sometimes impossible job for the regular teacher.

Special education teachers have chosen this specialized field of teaching while regular teachers have not. Special education teachers are highly trained, yet most regular teachers have never taken a course in special education... and may have no desire to do so. If a teacher has the desire to teach special education, he/she studies to become that type of teacher. If a teacher has no desire to teach special education students, this should be their choice.

Teaching special education takes more time than teaching regular students. All lessons must be modified expressly for *each* type of special education student. These modifications could include: preferential seating, a cooling off period, taped tests or worksheets, highlighting texts, typed handwritten material, giving directions in a variety of ways, shortened assignments, reduced paper and pencil tasks, avoiding penalizing for spelling errors, checking often for understanding, having students repeat directions, additional time to complete assignments, simplifying tests, or a combination of any of these modifications. Of course, all of these modifications are in addition to the teacher's other duties and responsibilities.

It is easy to see why the regular student is missing out on the assistance and attention of his/her teacher. There is just so much time and energy a classroom teacher has to give. The constant disruptions, discipline problems and educational modifications cannot help but have a negative impact on the standards and expectations of the class as a whole. Performance and skill levels are consistently lowered.

Teaching today is at a much slower pace for subject matter, but at an accelerated pace for paperwork, preparation, procedures, the rights of the special needs students, preparing for standardized testing, and the increased stress level of the classroom teacher. Absolute confusion reigns. And as a result, the average and above average students are slowly becoming the neglected and inferior group.

Code 504 students and special education students are allowed a "second chance" if they make a failing grade on a major test or on any other grade that has a major impact on a six weeks grade. This is called "remediation and reassessment." This means the teacher must make additional assignments and additional homework and re-grade, or let the student complete assignments that were never completed when first assigned. Regular students are usually not afforded a second chance. Why not let everybody do everything twice? Teachers, I'm sure, wouldn't object to even more paperwork. They love it!

Remediation is helpful for students who have worked hard and are still unsuccessful in making passing grades. Long before remediation became trendy for educators, teachers made allowances for these student's capabilities. Often it is the lazy, disruptive, or uncaring student who refuses to work, turn in assignments, or study for tests that teachers resent being forced to give a second chance.

Teachers are "encouraged" to pass all Code 504 students and special education students. In the long run, this is the wisest and easiest thing to do. Otherwise, if a student fails, a teacher must have in hand a complete documentation to validate why the student failed. These documentations include: What modifications were made? Why were they not successful? What could the teacher have done differently to insure success? And the documentation must be done on every student that fails. Talk about paperwork! Nowadays, grades in the grade book are just not enough anymore.

The buck always stops with the teacher and not the student. If a teacher must give a special needs student ten or more

64

extra points to pass a class, why shouldn't the teacher also give an A student or a B or C student ten extra points? Why don't we just do away with earned grades and give everybody an A+! It makes about as much sense.

Special needs students have many more rights than other students. For these students, there are special excuses for poor performance, poor behavior and the absence of responsibility. There is even a cap put on the number of days these students can be put in in-school suspension or alternative school. Teachers have lost all control over their own classrooms. And what happens to those special students if they reach the work force and are not treated differently from anyone else?

Questions we must ask ourselves: Is our goal for our special needs students to provide social enhancement or educational enhancement? Are we now providing them the education and training necessary to become productive citizens according to their capabilities? Or have we just thrown them into the mainstream because we believe that is where they belong?

As public schools continue to adjust standards for students and focus on the slow student, the disabled student, the special education student, the English as a second language student and the "at risk" student, we will continue to be bewildered by what went wrong with our public schools.

And what about the average and above average students and their rights? Aren't we discriminating against them?

Chapter Seven
And The Teacher Says
Over And Over And Over...

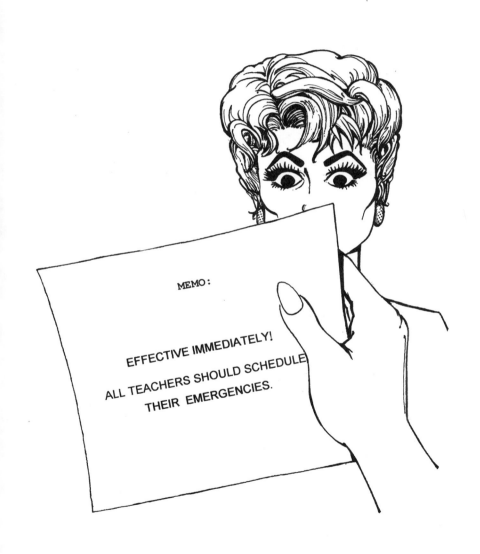

AND THE TEACHER SAYS
OVER AND OVER AND OVER.....

If you could be a fly on the wall you would be able to hear these utterances regularly in classrooms across the nation:

"I have *how many* students in my classes?"
"You mean we have *more* paperwork?"

***

"Will this day *ever* be over?"
"Will this week *ever* be over?"
"Will the Thanksgiving holidays *ever* get here?"
"Will the Christmas holidays *ever* get here?"
"I just don't believe I can make it until spring
      break!"

***

"Sit down please!"
"Sit down!"
"Sit!"

***

"Quiet please!"
"Be quiet!"
"Get quiet!"
"Quiiii...et!"

***

"Listen please!"
"Please listen!"
"Listen!"
"You are *not* listening!"

"I am *not* going to ask you again to listen!"

"Will you please listen?"

"Of course you don't know what to do, you were not
listening!

***

"Don't cry, go talk to the counselor about it."

"Don't cry, I'll help you open your locker."

"Don't cry, she didn't mean what she said."

"Don't cry, you can get another boyfriend."

"Don't cry, you can't control what your parents do."

"Don't cry or I'll cry too!"

***

"Do *not* call me 'Miss.' I have a name!"

"No, you can't go back to your locker!"

"No, I don't have a safety pin!"

"No, I don't have a Band-Aid or an ice pack!"

"No, I don't have change for a dollar!"

"No, you can't go to sleep!"

"No, I will not *just give you a zero*!"

***

"Yes, you may have a tissue."

"Yes, you may go to the restroom."

"Yes, you may get a drink of water."

"Yes, you may go to the nurse."

"Yes, you may borrow a pencil."

"Yes, we have to do that today."

"Yes, we are going to do something today. We do
something every day."

***

"Do not cough in my face, please!"

"Do not push in line!"

"Get rid of the gum!"

"You are not done! Hamburgers are *done*...you are
    finished!"
"It is 'may' I go to the restroom? Not 'can' I go to
    the restroom?"
"Because 'can I' means am I capable, and 'may I' means
    asking for permission!"
"The bell rings today at the same time it rings
    every day."
"I only told the class three times this week they were
    having a test today and *you* didn't know about the
    test?"
"We reviewed for this test yesterday for the entire class
    period and *you* didn't know we were having a test?"
"Don't you *ever* listen?"
"Can't you follow *one simple direction*?"

***

"We have to fill out *another* survey?"
"I have so many papers to grade I'll never get finished!"
"I'll be averaging grades until midnight!"
"I feel like a pie baked for eight and served to 124!"
"You mean we aren't getting a raise *again*?"

***

"Listen!"
"Pay attention!"
"Quiet!"
"I have such a headache!"
"Please Lord, get me through this day!"

"No! I will not just give you a zero!"

Chapter Eight
Some People Are
A Pain In The Class

DUE TO THE TORNADO THAT RIPPED THROUGH THE CITY
LAST NIGHT, ALL AREA SCHOOLS ARE CLOSED.
HOWEVER, TEACHERS ARE TO REPORT AS USUAL...

SOME PEOPLE ARE
A PAIN IN THE CLASS

PART I

States and the federal government make decisions that affect the lives of students, teachers and the educational process. They are not, however, qualified to make decisions for the teaching profession, nor should politics have a place in education. But politicians continue to run things. State and federal mandates have largely contributed to the serious problems facing public education today. Sometimes it is downright alarming to witness what comes from the powers-that-be!

Case in point: In August 1991, a state legislator from Houston, Texas voted for legislation three times in one day while the legislature was in session. There is nothing particularly unusual about a representative voting on legislation several times in one day, except that this House member *had died the day before!* It is scary enough when some of the elected officials in the state legislature who are presumably alive make important decisions, but it is just going too far when the dead ones are having their say, too.

The Texas House Speaker did acknowledge that while having a dead man vote with the assistance of another legislator is "embarrassing," he also had this to say, "It's hard to ride herd on 149 members of the House when you have to trust them and their integrity at the same time."

Now, if the Texas Speaker of the House cannot ride herd on 149 adults during a legislative session, how can he and his colleagues have the audacity to expect a teacher to: ride herd on 150 or more kids every day, follow absurd state legislation and local board directives, and educate students at the same time? Forget trust and integrity. All state legislators and local board members should be given the opportunity to ride herd on a wild and dangerous stampede mounted on a broken-down horse with no spurs on their boots, as teachers do every day in their classrooms. Talk about riding herd!

The people who have become a pain in the class can be found at the federal, state and local level. The enormous problems that confront educators are compounded by the impractical and unrealistic nonsense that is thrown at teachers year after year. If you can read, a teacher probably taught you. Why not ask one their opinion on any or all of the following subjects??

STANDARDIZED TESTING

Each year, until the latest standardized test presently in vogue is given, teachers must focus on "teaching the test." Huge sums of money are spent on test teaching materials...not to mention the actual cost of the test. More and more teaching time is spent preparing students for this test. Teaching for the test has become the Super Bowl and Academy Awards all rolled into one event.

The testing mania among administrators and school boards threatens principals with the loss of their jobs if test scores are low. And teachers are told to GET THOSE TEST SCORES UP OR ELSE! Rationality seems to be lost in the interpretation of what these tests are about. It is almost as if educators are actually taking the test and it is their success or failure being evaluated instead of the students.

Isn't it insanity for anyone to believe that we can determine a person's capabilities on a single test? Little thought or consideration is given to an individual's I. Q. or academic background. There are many variables and circumstances that produce low test scores. To hold teachers and administrators accountable for student performance on this test is absurd.

From the trenches, the echo is loud and clear:

"Unrealistic pressure is placed on educators to see that high test scores are achieved, because the scores look good in print. Instead of teaching curriculum subjects, countless hours are spent teaching the test format. Teachers are held accountable without regard to their student's academic background or capabilities or if a student attended that school the previous year, or twelve other schools." Lisa M.

"News flash! Test scores do not measure student learning and never did!" Richard W.

"Teachers know that test scores are useless as an academic evaluation, but the public continues to demand these scores as a measurement. Test scores are compared with other schools' scores in a community. School districts are compared to other districts and

state scores are compared with other states. The vocabulary on these tests is appropriate for children raised in a white or blue collar environment. So many children cannot measure up to such a vocabulary. This type of testing is like comparing little apples and oranges with big apples and oranges. Testing is not a true picture of learning, but these tests continue to become more important each year. There is nothing on standardized tests that will prepare a student for the job market or life. William Shakespeare summed it up nicely when he said, 'Much ado about nothing!'" Paul I.

"Testing has become a train rolling out of control. Everything hinges on test scores. They determine whether a student can graduate or attend college, or if a student can be in honors classes or the gifted and talented classes. They determine whether a student must take reading or not and the list continues. Testing has become the way to measure how well or how poorly an individual school and an entire school district is doing. These are all erroneous assumptions." Ester P.

"Given correctly, a test can serve many useful purposes and tell us much about where a student is academically. But they should not be designed to be the monster they have become." Gloria M.

"We are told there are no acceptable reasons for low test scores. We must take responsibility for all the different languages students speak with limited English. We are held accountable if students do poorly because they took the test while ill, or watched television half the night, or stayed awake while their parents fought. We are accountable for those students enrolled in school with low reading, math, or English skills and a limited vocabulary. There is no consideration given for low test scores that are the result of drugs, alcohol, physical abuse, or hunger. And for the students who could care less if they mark an answer right or wrong, we are held accountable." Jimmy D.

"The large and the small obstacles that are overcome after working for hours and hours with students is not measured on a test. The hard work of day to day teaching, tutoring, counseling and caring for students does not appear on a test. The student who has lost a parent, or lives in the same small house with ten other people, or cannot perform well on a test are only low statistics to the testing bureaucracy. Standardized testing determines only whether a student can pass a test. It has nothing whatsoever to do with an education. Testing is so popular among the fools who make the rules that now they are talking about a system of national testing which would be geared to "world class" standards. Proponents say the assessments would not only provide a better picture of student performance than currently exists, but would also establish high standards that would drive student achievement upward. POPPYCOCK! HOLD ON TO YOUR CHALK TEACHERS! ONE OF THESE DAYS IT LOOKS AS IF WE WILL BE TEACHING THE TEST ALL YEAR AND CUT OUT ACADEMICS ALTOGETHER!" Sandy J.

"The media accents the negative and overlooks the positive. When SAT scores go down, it is front page news. But when SAT scores go up, it is back page news. The media has been one of the most influential forces behind the 'testing craze.' Well hold the presses, we will get this year's test taught too!" Janie V.

A Texas teacher of 42 years had this to say about testing and all the other associated nonsense:

"The latest 'quick fix' educational innovation in testing is called TAAS which is pronounced 'toss', which is what should be done with it, and all the other modern educational 'miracle cures' such as TEAMS, TAB, SAT, ACT, etc., so that teachers could be left alone to teach.

The first year that I taught, in the 1940's, for which I earned $2,465 a year, I had a double major in English and Spanish. Teachers were assigned to teach English, math, science and social studies, regardless of their major. Textbooks were not provided, so we had to improvise. For math, I brought my grandfather's old arithmetic book, which worked reasonably well despite my limited mathematical acumen. But one day I encountered a word problem I could not solve, nor could any of the other teachers, including one or two who had been math majors.

I took the problem home to my mother and father who had a high school and eighth grade education respectively. Each one separately solved the problem within five minutes. How could they possibly do that without ever having had TEAMS, TAB, TAAS, SAT, or all the other products of miraculous progress in education, not to mention never having had the benefit of a school counselor or a calculator or a computer?

From all I could discern, people in those days were really taught with no sidetracks and with no education agencies to introduce *new and improved methods that very seldom work. I think we could teach now also, if they would leave teachers alone and throw out most of the modern techniques and close the education agencies. All in favor, say 'aye'!"*

STAFF DEVELOPMENT OR INSERVICE

Once in a great while, teachers attend an inservice that is beneficial and productive. However, the majority of inservice or staff development days force teachers to waste valuable time they could be using on preparation for students. Inservices are notorious for being boring and counterproductive. If teachers conducted their classes in the same way most inservices are conducted, they would be "tarred and feathered" and run out of town. Teachers detest inservices, but they seem to accept this as a fact of life like an occasional pounding headache or a bout of diarrhea.

There are three major reasons for inservice: (1) The state believes they are great and mandates how many a teacher must attend, for what amount of time, and more often than not, what the subject should be. (2) The people who mandate inservice do not have to attend and have either never been in a classroom as a teacher or haven't even been near a classroom since polyester leisure suits were in fashion. (3) Those in the bureaucratic chain of command have the opportunity to justify their existence by planning and presenting inservice.

Although staff development can be costly, here are a few suggestions for topics that might be of some value to teachers:

- IDENTIFYING AGGRESSIVE STUDENTS AND THEIR FAVORITE WEAPONS

- LEARNING THE SPECIAL MATH THAT CONVERTS STUDENT GRADE AVERAGES OF 50 OR BELOW TO A PASSING GRADE

- HOW TO BE A SOPHISTICATED SCAPEGOAT FOR THE ILLS OF SOCIETY

- COPING WITH BEING AN ADULT PROFESSIONAL WHO IS TREATED LIKE A CHILD, WORKED LIKE A MULE AND PAID LIKE AN INDENTURED SERVANT

- LEARNING TO LIVE WITH DIGNITY AT THE POVERTY LEVEL ON YOUR RETIREMENT BENEFITS.

Teacher comments on inservice include:

"Most inservices are a waste of my time and your money." Sarah B.

"I am a taxpayer along with being a teacher. The money spent on useless inservices should be investigated. Are the children benefiting from this direction of spending? How much are teachers benefiting?" Lois H.

"In the many years I have taught school, I can honestly say I can count on one hand the inservices that have been beneficial and worth my time. Invariably, I have ended these days mad and frustrated. My time is just as valuable as anyones and I could have used that time to much better advantage. Does anyone care what teachers think? No, and they never have." Helen F.

PARENT-TEACHER CONFERENCES

Teachers are always ready and willing to talk with parents who are genuinely concerned about their kids. However, the parents who refuse to listen to the facts are convinced their child can do no wrong and are disrespectful, rude and a thorn in any teacher's side. Teachers would love to tell these parents, " I suggest you take your kid home and teach him/her yourself!" But of course they can't.

Teachers are very verbal on this subject. To wit:

"Some parents have the mistaken idea that teachers are the enemy and out to get their kids. Nothing could be farther from the truth." B.L.J.

"The parents who want to help their kids think of the teacher as a professional. They treat the teacher with respect and are supportive in trying to solve the problems. We just don't see many of this type of parents anymore, but we are so thankful when we do." Jane M.

"Everyone in education now slinks around trying to be unobtrusive. You must defend yourself at every turn instead of being able to say, 'I made this decision for these reasons and I do have the right to decide this issue because I am the teacher and a professional.'" Larry H.

"It is so frustrating when parents allow their children to be habitually late or absent and back them by writing notes for excused absences. If that is not bad enough, every year or so, the state or the local board raises the amount of absences a student can have. This is like saying students don't have to be there, but you must teach them anyway. Sure makes a lot of sense to me!" Mary L.

"The parents and administrators that expect teachers to have a well-disciplined class but refuse to provide their support, leave teachers with a loss of effective respect, authority and control." Ronnie B.

"I have had so many parent conferences where the parents think their kid is the only kid in school and things should be done to accommodate their kid." Bess A.

"Many times a parent tells me, 'I can't control my child at home either. I don't know what to tell you. We took away his/her phone and television but it didn't work. 'But I am expected to control their kid and 150 or more others, teach them in the process and keep my mouth shut and not rock anybody's damn boat!" Beverly J.

ATHLETICS

Athletics has motivated many students to pass and has kept students in school. Coaches put in long hours and are under a great deal of stress, because a coach is only as popular as the score of his/her last game or winning and losing season. Most coaches work hard to teach self-discipline, self-esteem, persistence, fair play and the importance of an education. Few kids ever drop out of school because they don't like athletics. On the contrary, they usually stay in school because of participation in athletics.

There is another side to athletics and coaches. Some coaches are excellent classroom teachers, but teachers deeply resent the coaches who have few or no classes and draw much larger salaries. The coach who teaches one or two classes a day and is paid a salary of $52,000 to $62,000 a year is not too popular with the teacher who has six or seven classes a day, has a masters degree and makes $32,000 annually. Financial priorities have always been heaped on the athletic programs and if there are budget cuts, you can bet your bottom dollar the major cuts are not in the athletic department. The rationale has always been that athletic games and events brings financial compensation into the school district. Has anyone ever considered how much it costs a district or community in the long run when academics are short-changed financially?

Often, when a coach must have a particular subject to teach — many times this is social studies — experienced social studies teachers are moved elsewhere to teach another subject, so the coach can have the teaching assignment. And there is an unwritten rule in Texas: DON'T FLUNK AN ATHLETE IF YOU KNOW WHAT'S GOOD FOR YOU!

There also is a saying that sums all this up: WE WILL BE IN TROUBLE AS LONG AS WE PAY THE WORST FOOTBALL COACH MORE THAN WE PAY THE BEST TEACHER.

PRINCIPALS

There is nothing a faculty values more than an effective principal. They are completely devoted to the principal they respect. To earn that kind of dedication, a principal must put the students first and genuinely care about them. This is followed very closely by the treatment of the faculty with appreciation, respect and support. A good principal knows what teachers are up against in the classroom and listens when they have a problem, complaint or suggestion. The principal may not agree with their idea or solution, but an admirable one will at least listen and communicate with his/her faculty. If a principal cannot support a faculty member, who will?

Leadership qualities and "people skills" are a must for an effective principal. Sadly, public schools do not have an abundance of principals or administrators with these skills. A lousy principal can ruin an entire school when he/she does not have the respect of the faculty. Schools are sometimes filled with "good ole boys" and former coaches who have become principals because they belong to the "good ole boys" network. They remain principals even when they do a terrible job as an administrator. Some are so self-absorbed with administrative powers that they haven't the slightest idea that there is a right way and a wrong way to deal with people. This type of principal has little rapport with the faculty and has no idea how to motivate with any degree of leadership or verbal appreciation.

It is rare today when a principal truly knows or even cares what teachers are up against in the classroom. The word "support" to most male principals means a jockstrap.

The brotherhood of "good ole boys" is alive and well in public education. Indeed, Texas may have given birth to the original "good ole boys" network as it also extends into politics, big "bidness" and athletics...as well as school administrators. At one time, the state was awarding principals a cash bonus if their test scores went up a certain percentage. No, the school was not rewarded...the principal was. And do principals actually have anything to do with raising test scores? No!

TRAINING FUTURE TEACHERS

Our colleges send student teachers into public schools to "practice teach" with experienced teachers who, in turn, are paid very little or absolutely nothing for this service. This is another example, in a long list of many, of how teachers are expected to do another job for free, or far below minimum wage. Teachers have always been told it is their professional duty to train teachers for the profession. **WRONG!**

If a teacher, with years of teaching experience, is going to take the time and make the effort to train another person to teach by sharing years of expertise and techniques, he/she should be compensated for doing so. Potential teachers certainly cannot receive such training anywhere else. Student teachers will be the first to admit, **"Nothing I learned in college prepared me for the classroom!"**

Indeed, neither a college education or a military boot camp or a police academy can prepare a teacher for the classrooms of today. And certainly a college professor who has not been in a public school classroom as a teacher in twenty-five years cannot possibly prepare a teacher for combat tactics, endurance techniques and survival skills.

EVALUATIONS

When merit pay became involved in teacher evaluations, morale hit the skids. Favoritism, personalities and the moods of an evaluator cannot help but play a part and add to the unfairness of an evaluating system for teachers.

As any sane teacher knows, some evaluators are not knowledgeable about the subject they are evaluating and have no concept of how the subject should be taught. The "dog and pony show" that is performed during evaluations has very little to do with teaching on a daily basis.

One example of specific guidelines that teachers were

graded on in Texas at one point numbered anywhere between 50 to 80 different strategies that a teacher must accomplish in one class period to get a high evaluation. With merit pay involved, teachers scrambled to meet the evaluator's criteria. Then, Texas decided to do away with merit pay, leaving some teachers on a high level of pay (level three), some on a lower level of pay (level two) and some teachers at level one with no merit pay at all and no chance to ever receive it. No longer funded by the state, local districts either elected to continue funding merit pay levels or use the merit pay monies instead of giving raises to teachers. What is wrong with this picture?

If you examine the picture closely, you will observe the Texas bureaucracy at its very best! It is a fantastic model of HOW NOT TO DO IT!

To resolve educational problems, the state was gung-ho to evaluate teachers and give them merit pay for meeting certain criteria...namely high evaluations and the completion of additional college courses and/or degrees. In order to comply, every Tom, Dick and Harry along with every Mary, Jane and Carrie rushed to get the additional courses and complete their Masters degrees, whether they could afford it or not.

Then came the fun part! Teachers went into a sweat and panic each time they were evaluated. They anxiously waited to see if they had made the next level of the merit pay ladder. Some did and some didn't. Incidentally, we are not talking about winning part of the lottery. Level two paid $1,500 a year and level three $3,000. But this additional money looked good to everyone, especially those who hadn't received a raise in years.

All this isn't important now...at least not in Texas. However, I think of this period as The Bureaucratic Bull Shaft Period that seems to linger in Texas.

Today, Texas teachers are just evaluated, period. Merit pay was just another example of what the Texas bureaucracy does extremely well: **We will do it this way...now we will change it and do it another way...now we will change it again...and now we will go back to the way we did it in the first place.**

During the merit pay fiasco, a story circulated in one school that a fire was discovered in a student's locker. Someone shouted for help from a teacher standing nearby. The teacher replied, "Call a Level Two or a Level Three teacher! I'm not competent enough!"

There is a positive side to evaluations because they seem

to help some teachers become more aware of their methods of presenting materials. However, the negatives far outweigh the positives in the manner teachers are evaluated.

Teachers should, of course, be evaluated on their performance. Evaluations should be simple and to the point. All subjects cannot possibly be judged in the same way, nor can all teaching techniques be evaluated with one instrument. Today, evaluations seem to be designed to take creativity and individuality out of the classroom and replace it with uniform robots who will conduct their classes with an identical sameness.

Here are some teacher comments on the evaluation subject:

"What a waste! Evaluations require you to be an ... ˙tor for one class period just to please an evaluator. After ten years, why do I have to keep proving myself and with someone else's teaching strategies?" Juanita S.

"How can anyone possibly think they can rate a year's worth of work during a couple of evaluation sessions? It's ludicrous!" Ben T.

"Some evaluators were not the greatest teachers themselves and yet they are grading my performance. I resent it!" Jason L.

"There is such a waste of professional talent in schools! They continually try to push the 'stifle button' on creativity." Wanda D

"Some teachers cannot teach students, but they can put on one hell of a show to impress an evaluator." Chuck T.

"Why are teachers evaluated and never given the opportunity to evaluate administrators and the evaluators? Central administration cannot adequately evaluate someone they never see 'at work,' but teachers certainly can! Well, the reason is simple, they don't want to know the truth about their administrators. That might require them to take some action!" Joseph K.

Evaluations should be designed to observe teaching ability, creativity and rapport with students. They should not be used to determine if all teachers are doing the same thing in the same way according to someone elses guidelines.

There are all kinds of horror stories among teachers about the way they are marked down for their student's behavior. If there is one thing you cannot count on, it is the behavior of students. One never knows what they are going to do or say. The very idea of professionalism being evaluated on the behavior of a student shows the mental swiftness of those who are a *pain in the class*. Therefore, some teachers are forced to reward students if they "perform" well during an evaluation.

Too often, an excellent teacher is given low marks while a mediocre teacher receives high marks. This is due to Miss Mediocre being liked by the evaluator, whereas Miss Excellent is not.

Some schools consistently give high marks while other schools give consistently low marks. There is little appreciation or monetary compensation shown for the extremely hard task of teaching without adding insult to injury with an unfair evaluation based on some educational joker's evaluation instrument.

Lastly, the thorn in everybody's side is the administrator who is so self-important when evaluating others. But if the truth be told, he/she in many cases couldn't do a teacher's job if his/her life depended on it. The swiftness memory loss in the universe must be the administrator who once was a classroom teacher.

TEACHER ABSENCES

Administrators seem to take it personally when a teacher must be absent. Teachers are told they cannot be effective in the classroom if they are not there. As the kids today put it: **Well, duh!**

Leaving classes in the hands of a substitute is no picnic for a teacher either. Most teachers would rather not be absent because it is less trouble and hassle just to be there. Consequently, they often drag themselves to school...sick or not.

Although years of teaching usually leads to a fairly strong natural immunity for some, teachers do get sick. They are exposed to all types of diseases on a daily basis. They are coughed on, sneezed on, and yes, vomited on by students. They handle hundreds of papers with a variety of germs...some known and some unknown. New teachers, especially, find themselves sick very often.

School buildings are notorious for harboring mold, mildew, dirt, bugs and bacteria. If a teacher has no allergies or health problems when he or she begins teaching, only the lucky escape developing them. Regardless, teachers are often made to feel guilty if they are absent.

The list of reliable substitute teachers is becoming smaller every year due to the nature of the job and the low pay. Often, just a warm body sitting in a classroom all day passes for a substitute teacher.

PART II

Never have teachers in Texas been more affected by the dudes who are a "pain in the class" than in 1986. Although that was some years ago, it is important to relate because it is a prime example of the mentalities and political rubbish that governs the teaching profession. Anyone teaching in Texas at that time will never forget what was crammed down their throats by the bureaucracy and they **should** never forget. It was a major disaster of educational screw-up on the highest level.

Texas politicians came up with the bright idea that the problems Texas was having with students who were not learning or becoming school dropouts was *teacher incompetence.* Arkansas had come to the same conclusion the year before, so Texas followed suit.

The politicos had a test devised that they thought would determine whether a teacher was competent or incompetent. This test would, in turn, solve the major problems school children were having in Texas. No wonder Johnnie and Joanie couldn't read! No wonder Jack and Jill were dropping out of school! We obviously had a state bursting at the seams with incompetent teachers! LET'S HUNT THOSE INCOMPETENTS DOWN AND RUN 'UM OUT OF THE SCHOOLS!

The media had a field day! Headlines proclaimed: "CAN TEXAS TEACHERS READ AND WRITE? ARE TEXAS TEACHERS INCOMPETENT? TEXAS TEACHERS TO BE TESTED FOR COMPETENCY!" As families gathered together for nightly television, they were told how Texas teachers would be tested to determine their competency and whether or not they could even read and write.

Texas chose to forget the fact that these questionable "incompetents" had college degrees and years of teaching experience. Forgotten too, were the millions of students who had been and were currently being educated. Texas politicians in the state capital tossed the "big cow chip of misinformation" and ran with it. Under the enormous pile of manure were the teacher scapegoats who refused to believe that such a thing could be happening. But it was.

Texas teachers were officially informed that if they failed the test, known as the TECAT, they would lose their teaching credentials. They were sent booklets to study only to find questions that they couldn't believe.

Study sessions were held on school campuses everywhere in the state. Fast-track sessions were also available. One lousy screwball test would determine the livelihood of every Texas teacher. What other profession would have allowed such an outrageous display of political nonsense? None!

The following are only a few of the actual questions from the TECAT study guide which was almost identical to the actual test.

Taxpayers of Texas should have the opportunity to observe first-hand how their tax money was spent:

Adapted from a school board policy statement

It is the responsibility of the designated textbook committee to provide recommendations regarding the selection and adoption of student textbooks. These recommendations shall be submitted to the superintendent in the form of a report no later than March 1. The report shall be signed by all members of the committee who participated in the decision. After approval by the superintendent, no later than March 31, two copies of the textbook committee's report shall be sent to the School Board. This report shall be sent to the textbook division after the School Board approves it.

The decisions made in this report are final and cannot be altered during the academic year. During the year, teachers are encouraged to provide evaluations of the selected textbooks until February 3. Alternative textbook choices and reasons for their consideration will be considered by the following year's committee.

Question: *According to this selection, when must the textbook committee's report be sent to the superintendent?*

    A. during the week of February 3
    B. no later than March 1
    C. by March 31
    D. anytime during the academic year

Answer: B
Comment: Stimulating question! Requires a great deal of thought.

Adapted from an education journal

Goal-based evaluation, one of the more popular approaches to the evaluation of educational programs, has been used by American educators since the 1930's. Ralph Tyler, perhaps the nation's most distinguished curriculum specialist, was an advocate of goal-based evaluation well over 50 years ago. Goal-based evaluation calls for the evaluation of an educational program according to whether the program's goals have been attained. If its goals have been achieved, the program is judged positively. If its goals have not been achieved, the program is judged negatively. Despite its popularity, goal-based evaluation has a major weakness. There is no built-in appraisal of the quality of a program's goals. Thus, a program directed at trivial goals, or even unethical goals, could still be judged positively if those goals were attained. This is a substantial shortcoming of a widely used approach to educational evaluation.

Question: *Which of the following is the best statement of the main idea of this selection?*
  A. Goal-based evaluation has become popular among American educators only in recent years.
  B. Ralph Tyler is one of the nation's most prominent curriculum specialists.
  C. A major shortcoming of the popular goal-based evaluation approach is that the quality of program goals is not appraised.
  D. Many different kinds of approaches to educational evaluation have been used in the United States during the last decade.

Answer: C
Comment: Was this designed to bore the pants off of educators? It did!

Adapted from a memorandum

A norm-reference test was one of the tests used to place students into Advanced English.

Question: *Which of the following is the best definition of norm-referenced test as used above?*

A. *A test on which student's performance is compared to the performance of other students.*
B. *A test given prior to a particular sequence of instruction.*
C. *A test designed to indicate specific areas of a student's strength and weakness.*
D. *A test on which a student must earn a particular score in order to pass.*

Answer: A
Comment: Beneficial to competence in the classroom!

Adapted from a memorandum

Each innovative educational program must be subjected to a summative evaluation.

Question: *Which of the following is the best definition of summative evaluation as used above?*

A. *An appraisal of an educational program conducted primarily to modify and improve the program.*
B. *A careful review of the plans for an educational program prior to implementing the program.*
C. *An analysis and summary of the instructional resources needed to conduct a program.*
D. *A formal investigation of the effectiveness of an educational program.*

Answer: D
Comment: Isn't worthy of one!

Adapted from an education journal

School crime is a serious obstacle to public education. To cope with this problem, many students report avoiding areas on campus that are considered to be hazardous. Furthermore, some students avoid school altogether if they fear violent attacks or theft.
The disciplinary steps currently used to combat these problems are often ineffective. Temporary suspension, for example, may

aggravate the problem. Students who have been suspended fall fur-ther behind in their studies and become more prone to disruptive behavior. Discipline can reduce school violence, but only if it is fair, firm, and, most important, consistent.

Question: *Which of the following statements is an OPINION pre-sented in the selection?*

A. School crime has become the most important problem faced by schools today.
B. A principal's leadership style is the key factor in running a safe, law-abiding school.
C. Some students report that they stay away from areas at school that are known to be dangerous.
D. Consistency is the most important characteristic of discipline designed to reduce school violence.

Answer: D
Comment: This knowledge is invaluable to teachers
        in the solution of murder and violence
        in our schools!

Adapted from an education textbook

Several approaches can be used to help students learn to spell. For example, eye spelling involves memorizing how a word looks. This technique is useful for common words or words like "gadget" that are somewhat tricky.

Ear spelling involves spelling by the way a word sounds. It is helpful in spelling longer words such as Mississippi that are spelled like they sound. Ear spelling is used less frequently than eye spell-ing because many words in our language are not spelled the way they sound.

In hand spelling, the student physically traces the outlines of the letters in a word. This approach is used much less often than ear spelling.

Thought spelling has recently come to be regarded as the best strategy for teaching spelling. It requires students to associate the word with an idea that has already been learned. Unfortunately, teachers still use thought spelling less than any other strategy.

Question: *Which one of the following conclusions can most reasonably be drawn from this selection?*

A. Children who primarily use one strategy to remember how to spell words spell better than those who use several strategies.

B. Hand spelling is the best strategy for teaching spelling to young children.

C. Eye spelling is used to teach spelling more frequently than is hand spelling.

D. Eye spelling is not used very often because most words are spelled the way they sound.

Answer: C

Comment: This is typical of questions that served no purpose either in the asking or in the answering.

Adapted from a memorandum

To: *Students, Faculty and Staff, Watson High*
From: *Mr. Sundberg, Student Activities Director*
Subject: *Special Announcement*

Plan now to attend the regional championship basketball game between the Rams and the Lakewood High Lancers on Friday, April 19. The game, to be held at the arena, will begin at 7:30 p.m. Tickets are available at the Student Activities Office and are expected to sell out before the game.

*Several buses will be providing round trip transportation between the Watson student parking lot and the arena. The buses will leave at 6:00, 6:15, and
6:30 p.m. Because space is limited, seats on the first departure have been reserved exclusively for the basketball team and its coaches. Seats for cheerleaders will be held on the second bus, although additional seats should be available for faculty and other students. Because a relatively small number of bus tickets are available, individuals who want to ride the bus should purchase them as soon as possible.*

Come out and support the Rams as they play for the regional championship.

Question: *Which one of the following conclusions can most reasonably be drawn from this selection?*

A. Tickets for the 6:00 p.m. bus will not be sold to the general student body.
B. Basketball is the most popular sport among the faculty and students at Watson High.
C. The Watson High Rams will try to win their first regional championship title on April 19.
D. Seats on the second bus will be available exclusively for cheerleaders, players, and the coaches.

Answer: A

Comment: This one was a real favorite. Not only was it an insult to everyone's intelligence, it could have been written in a couple of sentences as could most educational memos.

Adapted from a memorandum

To: All Regular and Assistant Track Coaches
From: Chris Bell, District Athletic Coordinator
Subject: Track Conditioning Program

Below is a description of conditioning programs that are proposed for the track teams' practice warm-up. On Thursday we will select a program to use district-wide. The program selected must reduce injury risk by preparing the team for practice in 15 minutes without much fatigue. The programs under consideration are:

Program A: Two sets of 25 push-ups, sit-ups, and leg raises. Three 20-second intervals of four leg stretching exercises. A one-mile jog.

Program B: Three sets of 25 push-ups, sit-ups, and leg raises. Three 30-second interval of four leg stretching exercises. A one-mile jog.

Program C: One set of 30 push-ups and sit-ups. Two sets of 25 leg raises. Three 10-second intervals of four leg stretching exercises. A half-mile jog.

Based on past experience and recommended exercise rates, I have determined that program A requires 11 to 14 minutes to complete with modest fatigue. Program B typically require 20 minutes and causes considerable fatigue. Both programs A and B are sufficient to reduce the risk of injury. Although Program C causes minimal fatigue, it may not reduce injury risk because it is not sufficiently strenuous for warm-up purposes.

Question: *Which one of the following conclusions can most reasonably be drawn from this selection?*

    A. Conditioning programs B and C cause too much fatigue to be used for track practice warm-up.

    B. Conditioning program A is most consistent with the stated selection criteria.

    C. Leg stretching exercises are most important than push-ups and sit-ups for a track practice warm-up.

    D. The same number of push-ups are required in conditioning programs A and B.

Answer: B

Comment: Who wouldn't want their livelihood dependent upon questions such as this?

In Conclusion: These questions were only a sample of many that were on the actual test that lasted several hours. Is there a clue here why we have problems in education?

How did it all start? It started back in the summer of 1984 when the sixty-eighth Texas Legislature enacted House Bill 72. This bill called for Texas public school educators to pass a test as a condition for continued certification. All persons holding a Texas teaching certificate would be required to take a test and perform satisfactorily in order to keep certification and be eligible for employment after June 30, 1986.

Teaching certificates were suddenly not worth the paper they were written on and Texas legislators decided to change all rules of previous certification in mid-stream.

Few educators believed the testing would take place. THEY couldn't do that! It was illegal! Well, THEY could do that and THEY did do that!

On March 10, 1986, Texas educators marched into testing locations throughout the state to take the Texas Examination of Current Administrators and Teachers, called the TECAT. The test also had other names, none of which will be printed here.

It must be said that every Texas educator *should* have had the intestinal fortitude to refuse to take the test and march out together in protest. But they didn't. They had families to support and they had invested years in the profession.

To this day, it is still unbelievable that an entire profession would accept such unreasonable humiliation. If educators had rallied together, for once, and refused this kind of treatment, the state would have been hard pressed to do anything about it.

The whole insipid notion of the power of this test continued to smell to high heaven as being illegal...even after being challenged in court.

And if teachers had taken a hike, who would the state have hired to replace them? There were thousands and thousand of experienced teachers involved in this ridiculous assault on their personal and professional abilities.

An important question that should be asked: Could any of the legislators who passed this bill pass *any* simple competency test themselves? It's doubtful.

The proponents of the test were obviously not intelligent enough to know that teachers were college graduates with college degrees. And if higher education was awarding degrees to people who could not read and write, then competency testing should begin with the people running our colleges and universities.

Accordingly, if school districts were hiring people with degrees who couldn't read and write, their competency should have been tested. And if school principals were allowing teachers to teach for even one day, much less for five, ten, twenty or thirty years who had never learned to read and write, then those principals were extremely incompetent, to say the least.

It doesn't take an excessive amount of brain matter to know that it would be extremely difficult to complete four years of college and not be required to read and write, or show some degree of competency in the process.

When applying for a teaching position a person's competency or incompetency should be quite evident. To actually teach students and be able to fake competency is a feat that would make Ripley's "Believe It Or Not."

However, legislators were on a witch hunt for scapegoats. No doubt about it.

If any one profession is singled out as having college graduates who are questionable illiterates or incompetents, then shouldn't all professionals with college degrees be questionable?

To single out one profession as a possible blame for society's ills (with the absurd notion that its members may be incompetent) is inexcusable. INEXCUSABLE!

Incompetency is in our society and surfaces in all professions and walks of life. We find incompetency every day. There is no doubt that there are teachers who should not be in the classroom, just as there are administrators who should not be running schools.

There are surgeons who should not be in operating rooms and doctors who should not be in medical practice.

There are attorneys who should not be practicing law and certainly judges who should not be sitting on the bench. There are police officers who should not be on our streets. There are governors, state legislators, Congressmen in Washington, and yes, even Presidents of these United States, who have shown incompetency in their jobs.

Last, but certainly not least, there are incompetent parents who belong on the list. And the list goes on, because incompetency among human beings is a fact of life.

The Texas TECAT testing had nothing to do with competency in the classroom. Actually, the test measured nothing. Taxpaying educators were livid that their hard-earned tax dollars went to help pay for this politically motivated disgusting garbage. And they were equally as livid that the state had not given them a substantial pay raise in years.

Although Texas teacher's salaries were then, and still are today, on the low end of the national pay scale, the state could not afford decent salaries for teachers, but could afford to spend millions to test them on competency skills. Public school educators, at one time or another, had been called everything imaginable by students and sometimes parents, but never had they been called questionable literates...and certainly not as an entire profession.

The cost of the TECAT, depending on whom you believe, was between ten and eleven million dollars. Those millions were spent to find out if men and women with one or more college degrees and thousands of combined years of teaching experience could pass this test. The test...chock-full of tricky, inane, absurd and asinine questions *(and those were its good points)* served no purpose. IT SERVED NO PURPOSE!

According to published reports, 96 percent passed the test. Who knew if that number was accurate? Perhaps it was higher.

Who knows? Who cares?

One outstanding auto mechanic teacher in my school was so stressed about the test and the possibility of losing the job he loved, he died of a heart attack. The scare tactics used concerning the test were very real to him. Teachers who were the breadwinner of their family could not help but be concerned about the possibility of losing their livelihood. And that anxiety and concern included the highly educated and highly experienced, too.

When the test was over, teachers went back to their classrooms feeling angry and defeated. Many experienced teachers who could not be replaced were mad and disgusted enough to quit teaching and left the profession entirely.

Those behind the testing fiasco did manage one significant accomplishment with the TECAT. Teachers found that their credibility, dignity and professional pride had been stomped into the ground and their authority questioned by students in the classroom. Teachers were put in the unfortunate position of being ridiculed by students, parents and the news media. This issue has carried over into classrooms today and manifests itself with a lack of respect by students and parents. Makes one feel proud, doesn't it? Congratulations TECAT supporters!

Strangely enough, after the TECAT, students and parents continued to be apathetic. Students continued to refuse to take advantage of the free public education offered them... either by staying in school so teachers could baby-sit them, or becoming dropouts. More and more problems continued to surface. And today, we still have all the old problems and many new ones, with teachers once again being blamed for the majority of them.

As a footnote, in May, 1996, Texas Senate Bill 1 was passed allowing school districts to give teaching permits to anyone with, or in some cases without, a college degree. Supposedly, legislators did so to make it easier for districts to allow experts and professionals from every field to teach in the classroom.

As one legislator so aptly put it, "The concern was that you could have a recognized expert in, let's say physics, like Albert Einstein, and he couldn't teach in a Texas high school without jumping through all the rigors to get there. It was designed to allow the use of exceptional people."

Although THEY still don't recognize the fact that classrooms are already filled with experts and exceptional people, I personally doubt Mr. Einstein would consider teaching in any

Texas school for a couple of reasons. One, the low salary and thankless job, and two, the poor man has been dead for years.

The legislature is now allowing uncertified teachers in the classroom with what is politically referred to as "alternative certification." Because there is an acute teacher shortage due to migration, immigration, the baby boom and those who are disenchanted enough to leave the profession, "alternative certification" was put into force. This is going from one extreme to another, wouldn't you say?

To review: First we had the TECAT to rid schools of incompetent teachers and their certification. Now, we have a bill allowing uncertified teachers in the classroom. However, if any of them turns out to be an Albert Einstein or a Robert Frost or an Arturo Toscanini or a Marie Curie....I would love to audit their classes! In the meantime, I guess we will have to muddle through with what we have.

What is a good teacher, anyway? There are brilliant and well-educated people who cannot teach. There are those who are not brilliant, yet make outstanding teachers. There are teachers who don't know the difference between a dangling participle and the nominative case of a pronoun who are superior teachers. There are boring and unpleasant teachers who still manage to teach others. There are those who know their subjects backwards and forward, but don't have the ability to teach it to others.

There are those teachers who manage to stay only one step ahead of their students and can still teach with excitement. And there are those who can teach circles around everyone else with their enthusiasm and humor. TEACHING IS A TALENT. It cannot be measured by a test, or gauged and judged by another individual or evaluated by a piece of paper. A teaching talent cannot be duplicated or taught, or replaced, or bottled, but it can be shared. All of us remember at least one teacher who made an impression on us. And few of us ever knew how hard they worked, or the knowledge they had, or all the patience and caring involved. Certainly, we had no idea of the valuable contribution they made to our lives.

When we read, write, calculate, create, communicate, understand, question and work to discover answers, we do so because we were taught to do these things. Year after year we learned more and more until it all came together and we could go into the world and function and continue, hopefully, to learn.

(At least those who wanted to learn and worked to learn did so.)

It would be interesting to see the effect policy makers for education would have on other professions if they were allowed to govern them as well. Some of the following guidelines for physicians made the rounds in Texas schools with the author's name listed as "Ima Teacher." I was unable to determine the author to give credit where credit is due. As there was no copyright, I would like to share it and add a few extra guidelines of my own. After all, teachers have worked under these exact guidelines for decades. Perhaps, if these catch on in the medical profession, the legal profession might want to follow suit.

Teachers are not a selfish bunch and are very giving people who are always willing to share what they have.

GUIDELINES FOR PHYSICIANS

1. PATIENTS

A. All patients will be selected and sent to you by the state. You will have no choice in accepting or keeping a patient.

B. All patients will be grouped by age only. No consideration will be given to their individual problems or existing conditions.

C. All patients must make the same amount of improvement, in the same length of time, no matter what illness they have or how advanced their condition was when they came to you for treatment.

2. MEDICATIONS

A. You are responsible for assuring that all patients *enjoy* the medication you prescribe.

B. If a patient refuses to take the medication or participate in the treatment program or has no time to take the medication because of other interests, you are still held responsible for curing that patient.

C. If a family member disagrees with the prescribed medication or treatment, they must be placated. They are, after all, more knowledgeable about your profession than you are.

3. ADMINISTRATION

A. All decisions for a physician's practice will be regulated by an elected board. The only requirement for membership on this board is to have no knowledge or daily connection with medicine.

B. Your work will be evaluated for an hour once or twice a year based on what you accomplish during that hour only. The same criteria will be used for all doctors...regardless of their specialty.

    C. There will be a central administration office whose main duty will be to create paperwork for you to complete.

    D. Once each year, all doctor's patients will be given a medical test. The results of this test will determine your capabilities as a doctor. The test results will be compared with other doctors in the community and the community scores will be compared to scores within the state. The state scores, of course, will be compared with other states. All scores will be made public and you will be judged accordingly.

4. INCOME

    A. The state will determine your income. Your income scale will be decided during the last 15 minutes of the bi-annual legislative session. Any additional local funds may or may not be added to your income...if there are any funds left after the elected board has funded all other programs. Invariably, large raises are given to new doctors to attract them into the profession. Those who have remained in the profession thirty plus years will only advance financially by approximately $10,000.

    B. All administrators will make salaries much larger than yours, because their positions are more important than yours...the farther away one gets from patients the more the income.

    C. You will be expected to spend many hours attending various functions concerning your patients without being financially compensated. You also must contribute many hours of work at home for your patients free of charge.

    C. All paper work will be completed by you and you alone without benefit of secretaries or helpers of any kind.

    D. At retirement, you will live dangerously close to the poverty level...if not below it.

5. BENEFITS

    A. At the beginning of each year, you will be given a shiny new pencil, a highlight pen and a new calendar... depending on where you live.

    B. Health benefits are provided to some...depending upon where you live.

    C. After ten, twenty, or thirty years, you will be given a lapel pen in appreciation of your years of service...depending upon where you live.

Education should not be the complicated jumble it has become. If teachers would once again be left to teach their students, the following recipe would nourish and be enjoyed by everyone:

A SIMPLE RECIPE FOR AN EDUCATION

1 good teacher, well paid
A class of willing students, well behaved
A variety of books
A chalkboard and chalk
One overhead projector
Computers for each student
Software for each computer
Pens, pencils and paper for each student
1 or two loving and supportive parents for each student
A few supportive and empathetic administrators
(The last two ingredients are optional, but they make the recipe easier and more palatable)

Place the first two ingredients in a room. Close the door. Allow the ingredients to mix well. Add books, chalkboard and chalk, pens, pencils, paper and computers. Do not disturb. Leave to season for approximately nine months. During the seasoning process gradually add parents and administrators as needed. Be careful not to let mixture boil. Test, but do not overdo. When done, serves everyone.

Tip: This recipe has been used for many years with great success. The new ingredient — computers — enhances the recipe greatly. Otherwise, don't change the original recipe.

REMEMBER, TOO MANY COOKS AND TOO MUCH TEST-ING SPOILS THE RECIPE!

Chapter Nine
Lasting Laughter

"I'D LIKE YOU TO MEET MR. AND MRS. BATES

AND THEIR SON ... MASTER BATES!"

LASTING LAUGHTER

After years in the classroom, teachers often believe they have "heard it all and seen it all" only to once again be proved wrong. In the world of children anything is possible. Add parents, administrators and teachers to the mix and strange and humorous situations are bound to occur. A good "belly laugh" helps a teacher get through the day and retain his/her sanity.

The following incidences have been collected from teachers through the years and still bring laughter when they are told over and over again:

- Mr. George took his junior high history class to the library to complete a research project in conjunction with the study of the Civil War. After searching for some time, Mary Ester appeared frustrated and confused. When Mr. George asked her what the problem was she replied, "How do you expect me to report on Lincoln's Gettysburg Address when I don't know his house number, or his street, or zip code, or even the town where he lives?"

- The seventh grader checked out a library book with the title, *Unusual Animals*, for reading class. After staring at the first page several minutes with a perplexed look on her face, the teacher asked what was bothering her. She replied, "Mrs. Bentsen, what kind of animal is a Foreword? Have you ever seen one?"

- Students in physical education class were asked to write their answer to the question: How do you check your heart rate? Annie wrote, "To check your heart rate put your two fingers on your puss."

- The science teacher was explaining to the class that earthworms have two hearts, two stomachs, etc. Barry raised his hand and announced, "Oh yeah, you mean earthworms have multiple orgasms!"

- The first-year history teacher had some idea what she was up against when she told the class to take out two clean sheets of paper and number 1 to 10 on one of them. A student raised his hand and seriously asked, "Which one?"

It is always rewarding to find out how well students are listening in class...sure they are!

- It was a typical pull-out-your-hair day for history teacher Mr. Block. He is the one who found a condom on his desk and a sanitary pad on his chair. However, on this day while studying the War of 1812, he wrote these War Hawks' names on the board: Henry Clay, John C. Calhoun and Felix Grundy. The class period was spent discussing these men in detail and the fact that they wanted war with Great Britain. An indication of the class' attention came the next day when a student from his class walked into the room, glanced at the same names on the board and asked, "Mr. Block, is that a list of names for detention today?" *(Mr. Block's hair is gray now. It will take only a few more questions like this one to turn it white.)*

- After several days of discussion in class about the first Ten Amendments to the Constitution, a student raised his hand and declared, "Well, these certainly aren't the same amendments we learned at church!"

- Then there was the elementary school student, Dorothy June, who raised her desk top every day for a week and "threw up" in it. Dorothy June never told anyone, but after a week she didn't have to!

- One of the test questions in history class: Which group in the South was more democratic? Arnold wrote: "Vagina was more democratic."

- Mrs. Plumker was very discouraged while the class was studying World War II and she asked a student to give MacArthur's first name. Without hesitation the student, pleased with himself, replied, "General!"

- The high school teacher spent two days teaching her world history students about the Italians and their part in World War II. She placed special emphasis on Italy's leader, Benito Mussolini. His name was mentioned numerous times in the two days of lecture, discussion and films. On the third day the class was given a quiz over all the information. Question six: Who was the Italian leader during WW II? One student raised his hand and asked the teacher, "Can we just give the last name only for question six?" The teacher then announced to the class, "The last name is fine for question six." She received fifteen quiz papers with this answer: "The leader of Italy during WW II was Benito Fine". *(Now, would this be the height of frustration or what?)*

- The teacher asked her class to write a short paragraph on the topic: WHAT MAKES ME SMILE! One student pulls at the strings of the coldest heart when he wrote, "Don't nobody makes me smile. I am a ugly boy. You hate me but I don't care. I try to smile at you, but you look off. So what if I am ugly. I don't care and plus you don't care either."

- Another tear jerker was a sixth grader who had been abandoned by his mother and had to leave school during the day to go with a social worker and be put into another school. Many tears were shed by the faculty. As he left, he handed this note to his teacher: "Please don't cry no more for me. I will come and see you again. I love you. Do you love me? What is your fone number?" *(Sometimes, there are tears mixed with smiles.)*

- Three priceless sentences written by junior high students: Computers help keep cereal numbers on guns. Come Puters are very important because they help. Personal high jean should include a toothbrush and some toothpaste.

- Miss Lock, disgusted with her eighth grade class' behavior, asked them to write a paragraph on why they could not behave long enough to see a filmstrip. Each person was to explain why he/she misbehaved and why they believed their classmates misbehave. Matt summed it up very nicely when he wrote, "You just can't teach nothing to a bunch of dumb asses."

- The first-year eighth grade teacher only made this mistake once after asking a boy to read aloud to the rest of the class the note he had just written. He read, "Dear Connie, Jacob wants to know if you give blow-jobs and I do too."

- Big Joe was a constant troublemaker in his middle school. He was repeatedly escorted to the principal's office for his bad behavior and he always refused swats as punishment which were in use at the time. Instead, he always chose detention after school. One teacher finally had enough and hauled him to the office to receive swats..with no discussion. The principal raised the paddle, made contact with Joe's buttocks and Big Joe yelled, "Shit! My damn pants are on fire!" Sure enough, the impact of the paddle ignited the matches in his back pocket! Joe and the principal quickly jerked down Joe's pants and extinguished the fire. Although no serious damage was down to Joe's backside, Big Joe was never seen in the office again. From that day forward, the incident was known as THE BLESSING OF THE BURNED BUNS.

- And speaking of buns, unpleasant things happen at school all the time that teachers have to contend with. This one must top any list: Benny Bob had a serious problem. It seems that every day after lunch he would spend ten or fifteen minutes passing gas in the classroom. The other students would turn green and rush to throw open the windows and huddle in a corner at the furthermost point from Benny Bob. The teacher had repeatedly told him that this was unacceptable behavior, but Benny Bob said he couldn't help it. Finally, in complete desperation, the teacher called Benny Bob's mother to discuss the problem. She told his mother that this type of behavior could not continue as it was unfair to the rest of the class and to herself, as well. Benny Bob's Mother replied, "Benny Bob just can't control them farts. His butt is loose!" Now, what is a person to do? Well the teacher worked with Benny Bob teaching him "butt tightening exercises using her hand as an example. TIGHTEN, ONE...TWO...THREE...RELAX. TIGHTEN..ONE...TWO...THREE...FOUR...FIVE...RELAX, ETC. Benny Bob practiced and practiced and then one day he excitedly told his teacher, "It works! I ain't farting no more!" The class was extremely grateful, other classes and teachers were grateful and perhaps, all mankind should be grateful to this teacher!

- Ed didn't want to go to school. His solution was eating Ex-Lax every night and every morning so that when he arrived at school he would be sent home. Ed figured, and rightly so, that when one sits in the results of Ex-Lax in a classroom nobody is anxious to have them stay for the day. Weeks of counseling and threats resulted in Ed halting his solution. However, every morning Ed was questioned and then frisked to see if he was "packing" a box of Ex-Lax!

- The Repulsive Award certainly goes to the junior high student who had a definite statement to make the day he deliberately mistook the school elevator for a restroom. Just imagine a teacher's shocked surprise when the elevator doors opened and she found a considerable pile, topped off with a pencil stuck in the middle. Was it a #2 pencil, you ask? Only the custodian knows for sure!

- Miss Casper tells this story: "One day during my first year to teach, it began to snow. It snowed so hard that school was to be dismissed at 3:00 p.m., instead of the usual 3:30 p.m. I announced to my students that due to the weather I would not be available for tutoring after school that day. I explained to them, 'I will not be here today. I'm going home right after work before the weather gets worse.' One innocent and concerned seventh grader asked, 'Miss Casper, where do you work?'"

- Mrs. Beans was at her desk in computer class the day Buster, a quiet and well-behaved student, approached her and inquired, "Mrs. Beans, could I get out my dick...uh...oh...I mean my desk...I mean my disk!" *(Nobody can say who was the most embarrassed that day.)*

- Schools have become so overcrowded that portable classrooms — usually perched on blocks — have been purchased and set up outside main buildings. Mr. Pawley was busy teaching his eighth grade English class one fine day when the back of his portable classroom began to vibrate and squeak very loudly. Curious to find the cause, Mr. Pawley threw open a back window and stuck his head out to have a look around. Horrified, he discovered and eighth grade boy and girl leaning against his portable enjoying a few minutes of strenuous quick sex! *(Everybody swore that Mr. Pawley's eyes continued to bulge for a week!)*

- The orchestra teacher was busy as a bee conducting her orchestra class when her portable building began to move. Outside, movers were in the process of "jacking-up" the portable in order to move it to another location. Yelling at the students to remain seated, she made her way to the door, threw it open and screamed down from high in the air, "Would you mind waiting until we're out of here before you move this building?" *(After all was said and done, guess what? They were attempting to move the wrong building!)*

- Then there was the father who marched into the school building early one morning demanding to see the principal. On his head he wore a baseball cap with the words "OH SHIT!" When told the vice principal would be glad to see him because the principal was busy at the moment, he yelled, "I WANT TO SEE THE HEAD SON-OF-A-BITCH, NOT THE SECOND ONE IN CHARGE!" The principal, hearing the commotion, walked into the room introducing himself with, "How do you do sir, I'm the head son-of-a bitch you're looking for!"

- Mrs. Flautenhemer refused to let her son be paddled when he was sent to the office for cursing in class. She maintained that her son didn't know any curse words. Knowing full well he did, the vice principal gave the mother the choice of letting her son serve detention, or be given swats with a paddle. Mrs. Flautenhemer refused both options. *Her* son did not know any curse words or use curse words. Informed that the next step would be suspension from school for her son if she refused to let him be punished, she yelled, "Shit! My husband told him if he ever got kicked out of any damn school he would beat the living hell out of him!"

- The male physical education teacher was on duty outside during lunch one day when he told a female student to leave a restricted area. A few minutes later, she was back again in the exact same area. "Drop and do five push-ups," he told her. With a perplexed look on her face she did as she was told. The next day, the teacher was walking down the hallway and saw the same girl. Walking by her side was her identical twin sister! *(You got it! The innocent twin did the push-ups!)*

• The young and nervous teacher on her first day of school with a room crammed full of kids allowed a student to go to the restroom soon after class started. Ten minutes later, the girl returned and again asked to go to the restroom. "Are you sick?" the teacher asked. "You just went to the restroom." "No, this is the first time I have asked to go." she replied. Whereas the teacher announced, "I am not going to continue this conversation...go sit down!" As the class left the room that day, the teacher was standing at the door when the "restroom" twins smiled at her shyly as they walked out of the room.

• The drama teacher, frustrated and fed up with the constant talking during class, yelled, "Ok class, just piss your papers to the front of the room!"

• The very quite and proper English teacher was shocked to read this comment written by her principal on her evaluation form: "This teacher was very pissed with her students." After several days of worry and deliberation she finally asked the principal what she could have possibly done to cause such a comment. "I am so sorry," he replied. "This is a misprint. It should read, 'this teacher was very poised with her students!'" he explained.

• The Hilarious Award goes to this teacher: Mrs. Cain had the habit of calling her students Master So and So and Miss So and So. However, she no longer has this habit. Soon after the beginning of a new school year — during Meet The Teacher Night — Mrs. Cain was busy chatting with a couple and their son...one of her new students. Shortly, the principal joined the group. Mrs. Cain, using her most professional manners, introduced her guests to each other: "I would like for you to meet Mr. and Mrs. Bates and their son, Master Bates!"

Memos from administration are sometimes good for a laugh. One memo sent to the faculty from the principal raised a few eyebrows. It concerned some University of Dallas students who would be visiting the school campus.

Typing a "V" instead of the correct "U" can cause all sorts of questions.

MEMO: TO FACULTY V. D. students will visit the campus on 4/27. *(The principal was asked to explain what type of venereal disease these students had and why were they bringing it to our school!)*

Central administration has sent some great memos. A favorite faculty memo concerned who would notify personnel when the decision was made to close school during ice or snow days.

MEMO: CONCERNING BAD WEATHER DAYS The superintendent will ball the principals and the principals will in turn ball the teachers. *(Say What?!)*

The faculty had lots of fun with the following memo:

MEMO: TO ALL TEACHERS
FROM: CENTRAL ADMINISTRATION

PLEASE TRY TO SCHEDULE ALL YOUR EMERGENCIES BECAUSE IT IS EXTREMELY DIFFICULT TO GET SUBSTITUTES.

Well, teachers asked their family members to be considerate enough to be ill or even to die during the summer months only, or at least to have the courtesy to give a month or two notice in advance. *(How in the world do you schedule an emergency?)*

The Oscar goes to the memo concerning acceptable absences and also unacceptable absences which could result in a dock in pay. Perhaps the "i" and the "o" should not be next to each other on keyboards. What a surprise to receive this unusual memo!

MEMO: TO TEACHERS
FROM CENTRAL ADMINISTRATION

TEACHERS WHO ARE ABSENT BECAUSE OF BAD WEATHER WHEN SCHOOL REMAINS IN SESSION WILL RECEIVE A FULL DICK IN PAY.
(Wow! A good time was had by all with this one!)

Chapter Ten
Modification Mania

MODIFICATION MANIA

Second Period

As the tardy bell rang, Mrs. Porter closed her classroom door and inhaled a big gulp of air through her mouth and exhaled with a sigh. There had been no time after first period for a race to the restroom. Her mouth was dry and she was thirsty. Her head hurt. She would give a hundred dollar bill (if she had a hundred, which she didn't) for a cold drink with crushed ice. Instead, she settled for two aspirin and a couple of sips from her almost empty glass of warm water. It's only second period, she thought, and I feel like I've been thrown from a moving train. And this class is the equivalent to ten classes.

Jack, although an eighth grader, has a fourth grade reading, math and written language level coupled with a third grade spelling level. Mrs. Porter must follow these prescribed modifications for Jack:

- Use preferential seating
- Assign his work in smaller amounts
- Monitor his progress throughout class period
- Accept alternative forms of communication
- Pre-teach vocabulary
- Reduce length of exams or allow more time to complete
- Avoid penalizing for spelling errors.

Doesn't anyone understand how time consuming one modification can be, much less ten or twelve of them? No, nobody understands and nobody cares, thought Mrs. Porter.

Although Jack wasn't a serious behavior problem, he was lazy, lethargic and had to be pushed every step of the way.

Fred, on the other hand, is repeating the eighth grade and also has to have preferential seating. *How many preferential seats can one class be expected to have these days*, Sally thought for the umpteenth time. Fred has a third grade reading and math level and a second grade spelling and written language level. Mrs. Porter must highlight Fred's textbook and other materials, although the time and effort to do so is wasted on him. Fred was two weeks late entering school because he had been on his honeymoon. Still too young to drive, he had taken the bus.   His new wife Elsie, also in the class, was pregnant and frequently absent due to morning sickness. Fred was habitually absent, not because he was throwing up, but because he hated school. Fred and Elsie were expected to   drop out of school very soon. And in a few years, they will probably be the parents of five or six more kids and the cycle of behavior will eventually be repeated with their children.

Students crowded around Fred and Elsie telling them how lucky they were to be married. Two 15-year old kids married with a baby on the way and both still in the eighth grade. How unlucky can you get? What chance do they have? Fred is a Code 504. *(At-risk and a special education student)* Elsie is an average student.

Bobby entered school on parole after being in a car involved in a drive-by shooting. He isn't fond of school, his classmates or Mrs. Porter. It shouldn't be too long before Bobby is back in the "slammer" for violating his parole. He is arrogant, uncooperative and he is in school only because he has to be there. His hormones are cruising around his body at the speed of light and females are his only interest. Girls like him, too. Bobby is also a Code 504 and it will not surprise anyone if he fathers a child in the very near future.

No student in school holds a candle to Lawrence. Lawrence is Code 504 "royalty." He is known as "King 504" by his teachers. He came to classes equipped with a 22-page modification and behavior plan. His mother is the size of a bulldozer with a personality to match.   She refuses to realize that there are other students in the school other than Lawrence and she visits the school often to tell his teachers what they are doing wrong and how she wants things done.

Mrs. Porter now glances over the plan to meet Lawrence's behavior needs and the consequences for any inappropriate behavior he might display. Lawrence always displays inappropriate behavior. Mrs. Porter shakes her head in disbelief. A teacher with only Lawrence in a class would find it difficult to follow all of his modifications, much less a teacher with a room full of other students.

According to the written modifications, Mrs. Porter must give Lawrence a private cue to "cool off" should he become irritable or frustrated with no more than three cues per class period. *(Mrs. Porter must keep up with the amount of cues she gives)*

Lawrence also comes with this warning to the teacher:

Don't confront student in front of others or reprimand to embarrass him. Remaining calm works best, then follow these steps in order, after first calling his mother--which requires time out from her class to make the call or calls.

1. Verbal warning
2. Conference with student
3. Refer to counselor
4. Parent teacher conference
5. Time out for five minutes in hallway
If all these steps fail:
6. Send to office
7. Schedule *detention (Mrs. Porter gets to stay after school with Lawrence)*
8. In-school suspension *(but not to exceed five days)*

Mrs. Porter must also document Lawrence's behavior daily in order to cover her rear-end if his mother decides to sue her or the school district if Lawrence has low academic or citizenship grades.

DOCUMENT...DOCUMENT...DOCUMENT!

In Mrs. Porter's documentation report book she has written the following daily account of Lawrence's behavior for the previous week:

Monday: Lawrence wasted class time and hit a student quite hard in the back. Teacher talked to him about how dangerous that could be and that the student he hit had helped him with his work. Parent not called due to time element with only minutes until the end of the period and teacher was busy with instructions and answering questions for the other 27 students.

Tuesday: Several students helped Lawrence with his work. He was argumentative with these students about directions of the assignments. He said he did not care if material was spelled correctly or not. Verbally threatened several students and told them to "shut up." Teacher handled situation to the best of her ability as well as several other additional matters to attend to concerning the other students in the class.

Wednesday: Lawrence absent. Class relatively quiet.

Thursday: Lawrence asked for and was given help. Lawrence said he was finished with all his assignments. Teacher asked to see data on student's disk. Student did not have information on his disk, but admitted he had signed his name to another student's work which that student had allowed him to do. Both students received zeros for cheating. Teacher told the students how disappointed she was in them for cheating. Lawrence was not happy with receiving a zero and was afraid of flunking. He was told if he would get busy and do his own work and not cheat again, he would probably not fail. Instead of working for the remainder of the period, he chose to talk to another student and provoke him into an argument.

Friday: Lawrence had a comment about everything that went on in class today. He was asked to be quiet and get busy. Praise was give for work completed, although it is difficult to give praise when a student is a constant disruption.

And for today Mrs. Porter writes in her book:

Monday: Lawrence took a student's coat and wouldn't give it back. Caused several minutes of disruption. Then asked to go get a drink of water and was refused. Lawrence was furious and came to teacher giving dirty looks and mumbled under his breath. Class gave teacher a "thank you" card signed by all the class except Lawrence. He said, "I'm not signing any card for any teacher." He said it rudely and meant it to be rude. (Lawrence is a rude person. Lawrence's mother is also a rude person.)

Although Lawrence's skill levels are at or near grade level, there is page after page of modifications for him because he comes under the 504 program. And Code 504 students are not to fail! The following are only a few of Mrs. Porter's modification for academic success for Lawrence:

- Reduce distractions in the classroom.
- Re-position student's desk to reduce distractions.
- Provide individual help in organizing work and getting started.
- Change tasks frequently and prepare student before any changes in routine.
- Use peer tutoring.

- Allow student sufficient opportunities to release tension and discuss feelings.
- Reward student for making positive statements about self and others.
- Plan activities that demonstrate student's strengths and interests.

One can only imagine what this student and his mother will encounter when Lawrence attempts to step out into the real world. In the meantime, Mrs. Porter and all of Lawrence's other teachers — throughout his school years — must devote exclusive class time to this student, make sure he passes and doesn't physically hurt anyone in the process. There are many students like Lawrence attending public schools. And what about the irritability and frustrations of the teachers and other students who must cope with these students? There are no modifications for them, nor are there any concerns.

Wanda, on the other hand, gets right to work on her assignments. Since learning to type in Mrs. Porter's class, she is very proud of her accomplishments. Everything Wanda does is exceptional. Mrs. Porter wishes she had more time to devote to the Wanda's at Everywhere Junior High.

David, a special education student, works hard every day trying to complete assignments correctly. Although he is much slower than some of the other students, he puts all his time and effort into doing his best. Never a behavior problem, David is another student who could use more of Mrs. Porter's time. She tells him often how proud she is of him. On her way to discipline other students, she tries to pat David on the back as she walks by his desk. David gets a lot of pats on the back because this class has lots of discipline problems.

As this class winds up for the day, Mrs. Porter talks about the day's assignment which has been a job simulation involving a punctuation and spelling typing test on the computer. Mrs. Porter again stresses the importance of correct spelling and punctuation of the written word. Two students mumble it is all a waste of time and says "What is this anyway, an English class?" As the bell rings to end class, Joe announces he didn't complete his assignment. "Just gimme a zero!" he tells Mrs. Porter. Two classes down and five to go.

Mrs. Sally Porter...to be continued.

Meanwhile, down the hall, Annie Burton has her own set of problems. In the course of her day, this regular classroom teacher who is completing her 35th year of teaching has average and above average students in the same classes with these students:

- A child who has ADD (Attention Deficit Disorder) and Tourette's Syndrome.

- A mentally challenged child who cannot read or write or speak clearly.

- A special education student whose father is going to prison for murder; whose step-father died of a drug overdose and whose mother is a former prostitute.

- Two non-English speaking students.

- Two students who speak very little English.

- A student who is a felon. He stole several cars and is back in school after six months in a juvenile detention center and then under house arrest. He is also the father of a baby girl. This week, however, he was once again arrested for stealing another car and was sent "away" for the remainder of the year.

- Two special education students: One who wears the same clothes for a week or two at a time and does not bathe; the other who sits at his desk and stares. He doesn't talk...just stares. Both of these students love to read but cannot "connect" with other classmates.

- A student who is under a psychiatrist's care for ADD and emotional problems. He was expelled from a private school and is currently taking three different medications prescribed by his psychiatrist. This student habitually smiles all the time and blows kisses.

- Two deaf students. One is very shy and physically handicapped. The other has run away from home four times in twelve weeks.

115

- A student who is just out of drug rehab after abusing several different kinds of drugs. He writes morbid stories and loves the KKK.

- Another student who has just returned from drug treatment and whose mother is in drug treatment.

- A student who has dyslexia and ADHD. (Attention Deficit, Hyperactivity Disorder)

- One student who called Mrs. Burton "You old bitch!"

- And another student who called her "An Old Hag!"

Mrs. Burton is retiring this year.
Do you wonder why?

Chapter Eleven
Out Of The Minds Of Babes

"DON'T CALL ME AGAIN!
IT'S <u>YOUR</u> RESPONSIBILITY
TO CONTROL MY SON, BILLY!
. . . WHAT DO WE PAY YOU FOR?!"

OUT OF THE MINDS OF BABES

Middle school students were asked to complete sentences in their own words as a lesson in self-expression. They wrote the following: *(The thoughts and spelling are their own!)*

TEACHERS ARE.....

...sometimes nice, but alot of them are kind of strange.

...army captains and are all old.

...important to your outcome in life.

...people that teach students to be smart and are underpaid.

...a big help but some are knot.

...people who teach stuff.

...ugly, stinky, stuck up and ignorunt.

...the most prettiest people in the world.

...usually boring, life is boring and I am boring.

...mean and gripy human beings who are a pain in the necke.

...very boring and goofy.

...great because they help you start your life.

...just hard working men and women.

...grate most of the time.

...beautiful people and without them everybody would be stupid.

...people who explains stuff and helps everyone who has trubble.

...dull and upset.

...ok but their mean, obnoxious, bossy, and allways hurry you up.

I WISH.....

...to have world piece.

...my father would get back with my mom.

...my parents wouldn't get a divorce.

...I could go to a good colegde.

...I had a real fansy car.

...I could go to the Navy write now.

...my parents to come back because they are both dead.

...that school was never invented and teachers would kill
   theirselves.

...my parents would treat me like who I am and not who I was.

...my parents would get off my back and make more money.

...my parents would quit fighting.

...I would be richer than Mr. Walmart.

...that people didn't have anything against color or where you
   come from.

...my parents would dye.

...my parents wood shut up.

...my parents would croak.

...everybody in the world would be peaceful and happy and I could
   have the girl I like, and I could give my mom and dad what
   they wanted.

SCHOOL IS.....

...a bummer.

...a good place and about the only place to get an education.

...sorry.

...dum.

...sometimes a bour especially on Mondays.

...a waist of time!

...unnecessary

...a place to pass the time away.

OTHER GEMS

I am...not conceeded.

Life is...the most precious thing you will have.

I am...the most important person I've got.

I think...the world is crule.

At my house...people act like I'm not there sometimes.

I admire...my boyfriend because we have gone through hard and
    soft together.

The future...is doomed.

Life is...crul and I don't like it.

I am...sad all the time.

Life is...boring.

I am...not so pretty.

The future...is as bleak as a foggy day.

Life is...peaceful

I am...a Christian.

Life is...mean and unpredictable and boring except for Friday
   nights.
Life is...sometimes hard but it is all worth it.
I am...beautiful, kute, nise, braney, smart.
I think the world is...flat.
I think...kids flunk because they are dum.
Kids misbehave in school because...they do not pay a tenschin.
Kids misbehave in school because...they need a good spanken.
The world is...a mad house!
Parents are...seriously out to get me.
I think the world...is a beautiful place to live on.
The future...is something that ain't happened yet.

A class of seventh graders completed the following sentences. Sometimes there is pain and desperation in the minds
and hearts of children. Perhaps it is a miracle that some of
them learn at all.

I AM THE ONE WHO.....

...is grateful I have a stepdad that love me as if I were his own.
...can't ever seem to catch up with everybody else.
...never tries to be himself but always a combination of others.
...is the cheerleader with all the clothes and "the looks" and no
   dad.
...is insecure and very lonely.

...is popular and has it all, but who can't understand why.

...eats and eats and eats.

...is grateful I am alive.

...can't understand why my stepdad drinks so much or why my mom stays with him.

...wishes she didn't look like her father who is dead so she wouldn't make her family sad when they look at her.

...wishes she could cry without being thought of as a baby.

...my mother doesn't get along with.

...is afraid of living and afraid of dying.

...tries my best to love others but feels that they never love me back.

...wonders if my daddy loves me, since he won't talk to me and I haven't seen him in a long long time.

...misses my mother.

...tries to be like everyone else, but it never works.

...tags along behind when everyone else runs ahead.

...wants to be accepted but the only time I am is when somebody wants something.

...whatever I do is not good enough.

...wonders why I am even here.

...has the bad haircut and yellow teeth.

...has the ugly green carpet.

...always has family problems and can never solve them.

...feels left out of conversations.

...still sleeps with teddybears and is afraid of the dark.

A seventh grade Asian student new to this country and the language had a great deal to say on the same subject. If only we could bottle his thoughts and feelings to medicate the world:

I AM THE ONE WHO...

...cries.

...sings.

...never want to die.

...enjoy life and is happy to be alive.

...wish that the world would be in peace forever.

...wants everybody to be nice to each other.

...wish for true friendship.

...think people are sometimes crazy, yet...

...still loves everybody.

...think people should love one another just the way they are.

...wants a good life.

...wants to please my parents.

...wants my country to be free, and best of all...

I am the one who is glad that God loves me!

One day, as I watched my students while they worked, I wrote this poem of observation.

ANOTHER YEAR

They walk through my door for another year,
Some with eagerness and excitement and some with fear.
All those eyes are watching me and I know,
If they are to listen and learn I must put on a show.
From what kinds of situations have they come to me?
Are they wanted and loved or is there a hurt I can't see?
I spend the days and months teaching the things I should.
I would shield them from hurt if there was a way I could.
Their eyes are innocent, some are wise and others sad.
When I see the abuse and neglect it makes me mad.
Do I make a difference, have I helped the kids I teach?
Why are there more and more I just can't reach?
Do they see the defeat I often feel during the time we spend?
Do they know there are days I think I will never make it to the end?
But that day does come when we say goodbye and some even shed a tear.
And I know that others who need me will walk through my door again next year.

Chapter Twelve
Happiness Is An Asian Student

"THAT'S <u>NOT</u> WHAT THE TEACHER MEANT

BY ADOPTING ASIAN IDEAS ON EDUCATION!"

HAPPINESS IS AN ASIAN STUDENT

Asian students who have not become too Americanized in school behavior and academic performance make teaching the rewarding experience it should be. Rarely are Asian students not concerned about their grades and behavior. These students give teachers their full attention, they follow directions, and they are polite and conscientious. They complete homework assignments and are prepared for tests. They take pride in the caliber of work they complete and they have the desire and ambition to excel. Their behavior and manners are usually superb.

Many Asian students came to this country from countries ravaged by war, unable to speak our language and yet, they often surpass American-born students. Whether they came from these situations or were born in the United States to immigrant parents, it seems to make no difference in their ability to excel. No other racial group comes close to the Asians in their academic profiles.

Are Asians smarter than the rest of us? Do they have higher IQ's? Studies in the United States, Taiwan and Japan show there are no significant differences in IQ's. So what makes the difference?

One answer is a stronger work ethic that comes from strong family and educational systems. Asian-Americans are largely influenced by the ancient teachings of Confucius. Confucius taught that the order of activities for the superior person was:

- To improve himself
- To improve his family
- To make his country prosperous
- To make the world peaceful

All in all, certainly not a bad way to live one's life. Our American culture could profit from such teachings.

In a Confucian society, the teacher always has an honorable standing. Confucianism ranked the teacher just below the king and the father of the family. This spirit remains in their schooling and in their culture today.

Teachers are held in such high esteem that when a teacher enters a room in Asian countries, students rise to show respect. Asian parents feel that the teacher is the expert and that it is inappropriate to tell the teacher what to do. Hence, they do not participate in school affairs in their homelands. These parents sometimes have difficulty understanding our PTA or any other parental involvement.

Asians expect nothing less than the very best from their children, because education is perceived as their only method of upward mobility. There is a great amount of pressure on Asian children to excel, because traditionally, children are shamed when they do not excel. Not to do well brings shame to the family and to their ancestors. All of these ideas can be traced back to Confucian theories.

Strong support and consistently high expectations from the family are not the only reasons Asian-Americans do so well. Consider the educational systems in Asia and Indochina.

Japanese classrooms are strictly controlled. Students are greeted formally before and after each lesson. These greetings are then returned by the students. That should set a respectful tone for the day in any classroom. Students do not move around the classroom freely to sharpen pencils, or go to the restroom, or to their lockers for forgotten books. Off-task talk is rare. Students do not move from class until formally dismissed by the teacher. Furthermore, other teachers, supervisors, or administrators would never interrupt another teacher's lesson. This is in definite contrast to the average classroom management in America.

American students often resemble a herd of elephants when entering and exiting a classroom. And American teachers learn very quickly to teach around interruptions and disruptions. Flexibility and endurance is the name of the game if you are a teacher in American schools today. To be treated with honor is almost unheard of and to be treated with respect is rare.

Looking at the Asian curriculum, it is easy to see why students do so remarkably well. Students spend an average of eight to twelve hours a week on mathematics alone. Many students attend one-half day of school on Saturdays.

Asian attitudes concerning family, education, learning style self-discipline, and their respect for others are just a few of the lessons we can learn from them. Other factors to consider are their respect and thirst for knowledge. Sadly, many American students seem to have lost, or never learned, these attitudes and attributes.

Several Asian students were asked to express their views on the part parents play in a child's education.

This is what they had to say:

"It's a disgrace to this country the way kids act these days. They have no respect for adults, and they have no cares in the world. They do not realize that when they get older no one is going to support them. They all think school is a big waste of time; thus, they engage in conversations and fights instead of conserving their future. Furthermore, they take advantage of our freedom and this country. Only in America can a student yell to a teacher, 'Hey Miss', or 'What do you want?' without suffering grave consequences.

It is sad to see students make a travesty of the Pledge of Allegiance. While we are suppose to give thanks for our freedom, students throw candy at each other and make rude comments during the Pledge. I feel that two things are responsible for their behavior: the parents and this corrupted society we live in are the main causes. Parents are their kid's idols and they will follow in their footsteps, but society's influences is something everyone can fix. If these kids are the future of America, the future doesn't look so good."

***

"I believe that parents play a major part in their child's education. Although it is up to the student to want to learn, the morals and beliefs are introduced at home. A child often tends to take on his/her parent's opinions, therefore, parents should be very careful. They must show an active interest in their child's education by meeting teachers, explaining and helping with homework, and encouraging that desire to learn."

***

A Korean student wrote, *"My parents want me to have fun, but they stress education more than having fun."*

***

A student from Cambodia wrote, *"My parents want me to behave well because it is a rule in my family. I don't want to cause any more hardships on my parents by getting in trouble at school. I don't understand why some students misbehave in class because all it does is disrupt the class and disturb everyone."*

***

"It's a disgrace to your family to misbehave. We are taught from an early age to respect our elders. My parents taught me that you have to take responsibility into your own hands if you're ever going to make it."

***

And a young man from Cambodia wrote, *"The reason I go to school is I want to get an education so I can be somebody special. Success is very important. My parents came to this country so that I could have more opportunities and wouldn't have to struggle like they have. That makes me want to try harder."*

The following essays written by Asian students at the junior high school level should be a lesson for all of us.

THE NIGHT THE RIVER TURNED RED

I would like to tell you about my life in Laos and how I got to Thailand before I came to America. When we still lived in Laos, the communists were all over our country. They surrounded Laos and life was hard and not many foods to eat and hardly any money to spend.

My family and three other families decided to go to Thailand where we could have our freedom. The journey was very hard. We had no transportation. We had to go by foot. There was little food and water. We crossed many rivers. I thought this would be fun to do, but it was not fun to my father or the others. For awhile, my friend and I enjoyed it very much.

We all finally made it to the main river, but the danger wasn't over yet. We had to swim across the river between Laos and Thailand. The river was half a mile wide. We could not swim in daylight. We had to swim in the dark. We took turns, two persons each time.

When it was time for me and my friend to go we swam under the water as much as we could, because if we came up the communists might see us. But my friend did come up and the communists saw him. He tried to go down, but it was too late for him. They shot him in his back and the river turned red.

It wasn't fun anymore. It was a deadly game. I went down under the water and I heard the communists on the boat laugh at my friend. I said to myself if I only had a gun I would kill them all. Then they went away. I started swimming again toward Thailand.

When I got to Thailand I had to tell my friend's mother that her son had been shot and killed. I could not bare to see her cry, so I walked away. I thought I would never make it. But now we are in America, the land of freedom.

THE LIGHTS OF AMERICA

After many months in a refugee camp in Thailand, me and my family sailed into New York harbor right before Christmas. We saw beautiful lights of all colors! We could not believe what we were seeing. It was the most beautiful thing we had ever seen in our lives. We thought all those colored lights were there all the time, we didn't know they were for Christmas. I will never forget that first sight of America and those lights still shine for me in my new home.

AMERICA THE BEAUTIFUL

America, what a wonderful name this is. Even the sound of it makes a person feel at peace with himself. Just the mention of this beautiful land makes a person want to be free and liberated. This is the country for people of different races. It is a land where freedom shines through every city and town. This is a place where people can do as they wish without fear. It is a land that has done well within just a few centuries. America is a land where people wish to do well and strive hard. America to me is very important. This land has helped my family many times. America has provided us a place to live without fear of war. It is a place I hope to stay for as long as I live. This is where peace is its main domain. This great melting pot will always remain as a free nation for all want independence and liberty. America to me is a great country.

MY AMERICA

What does America mean to me? There are too many words to describe and too many things to tell. It means a great deal of freedom to me. After leaving Laos, I never thought I would be free and safe. Even though I was young, I remember a lot of things. America was a whole new world to me. I had to start out fresh and new. There was a new culture, new people and a new language. I thought people were crazy. They spoke a language I didn't understand and I spoke

130

a language they didn't know. But soon we became friends. As I grew up to be a teenager, I found out that there are millions of people just like me. These people searched for freedom, too. I am very happy and proud to be one of those people. When people ask me why I would like to stay in America, I tell them that it taught me the word FREEDOM. I am really happy where I am and very thankful. When people ask what America means to me, I wish they could read my heart.

Surely, we in this country do not have to go so far as to lose our freedom before we appreciate what we have. Our young people must somehow be made to once again develop a respect and appreciation for all that they take for granted. They must understand that America — the land of plenty, freedom and opportunity — did not just appear one day. For what we all enjoy, others have paid an enormous price. And can we keep what we have if we become a nation of uneducated and complacent citizens? Can a society survive the future with an abundance of apathy, ignorance, drugs, crime and immorality?

One Asian parent had a rule that his children didn't eat until all homework and studying was completed. In contrast, how many parents in non-Asian American families have to beg, or bribe their children to do their homework and study? Better yet, how many parents ignore their children's homework and studies?

It takes much more than a village to raise a child. It takes parents —very early on —to teach children responsibility, respectability, pride, ambition, and self-esteem. Otherwise, the village and the nation will suffer the consequences.

Children at school sometimes have disagreements, fights and disruptions concerning racial issues. And many a child has had hurt feelings over racial slurs from other kids. After one particular unpleasant situation, I wrote this poem to read to my students.

FACES

How is it possible there can be so many faces?
And who could have made them in all colors of races?

Look around at the diffent faces you see.
Each is made with the same things as you and me.

A forehead, eyes, cheeks, jaws, a nose and a chin,
And lips, ears and hair, on both women and men.

Count them, thirteen ingredients go into each face that is made.
That face is then covered with skin of a beautiful and different shade.

How can those few parts be made in such a variety of ways?
Who could form them in about the same number of days?

It seems impossible that each and every face born is new.
Does it just happen, or something someone would intentionally do?

Sometimes we are unkind to other faces while we are near,
And we cause them pain, suffering and fear.

What can be done to make all the world's people see,
That everyone is just the same, like you and like me?

Perhaps the answer may be as plain as the noses on our faces.
All of us were molded by just one loving creator of all races.

Chapter Thirteen
American Priorities

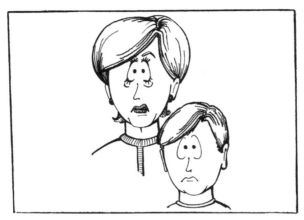

PAID: $26,000 TEACHING
TO SUPPORT MS. JONES AND ONE CHILD

COSTS: $36,000
TO TAKE CARE OF BIG DUKE

AMERICAN PRIORITIES

We put our financial priorities in very strange places in this country.

Remember when Mike Tyson made $22 million in 91 seconds using his fists and Michael Spinks made $13 million in those 91 seconds just for being on the receiving end of Mr. Tyson's fists? Remember when Deion Sanders signed a contract to make $35 million in five years playing football? Sports contracts boggle the mind and the pocketbook. Movie and television stars command millions for their talents. And their talents bring in more millions from all of us.

Then there is the other end of our priorities:

Catherine L. has a Bachelors and Masters degree and is considered to be an outstanding social studies teacher. She is a single parent and after 22 years of teaching takes home $1,800 every month. She works in a school district that has higher salaries than most. On weekends and during the summer months she mows lawns, hangs wallpaper and paints houses to make ends meet. Catherine L. could earn $22 million just like Mike Tyson, but she would have to continue teaching for the next 1,222 years.

Meet Marvin. Marvin is a "drug stasher." He holds drugs for dealers and earns up to $500 a day. Marvin, who has no degree and doesn't need one, influences young lives in a different way than Catherine L. does as a teacher. Assuming Marvin takes Sundays off, he takes home $13,000 every month and his annual income approaches $156,000. Marvin pays no taxes.

Mary S. has 23 years of teaching experience. Also a single parent of two, she has no savings and no investments. She nets $2,154 each month. Marvin, stashing drugs, makes approximately $392 more every day than Mary S.

Tommy is only twelve years old and works as a "look out" for crack dealers. If he "looks" for eight hours, he makes $150 a day. This twelve year old makes $5.25 more every hour than Mary S. does teaching school.

Jane K. has taught 28 years and has a son who completed only one year of college. As a salesperson, her son makes several thousand dollars more a year than his mother, receives a yearly bonus and has the potential to make a lot of money in the future. He has worked only one-fourth as many years as his teaching mother. At retirement, she will receive $1,895 a month...before taxes and insurance. She will have to find another job to supplement her retirement. In the past 28 years Jane K. has taught approximately 8,000 to 9,000 students and greatly influenced a few lives in the process. She has never received a bonus nor has her profession afforded her the opportunity to ever make a great deal of money.

Jasper is a "guard" and makes $300 to $500 in a single night guarding the places where drugs are sold. No particular training or education is required. No taxes are paid.

Last year, Pam B. taught school 12 months of the year, which included teaching summer school. She is the head of the English Department and has 23 years of teaching experience. Pam B. made a whopping $35,000 last year for all her efforts and paid taxes on that income. Although her experience is invaluable and it will be extremely hard to replace her, she is leaving the profession. The country in which she lives puts no particular monetary value on the services and talents of her profession.

Mike J. is 42 years old and has taught school for the past seven years. In addition, he coaches girl's athletics. His yearly salary amounts to $26,000. He is currently looking for another line of work to keep pace with inflation and mounting tax bills.

Stephen R. is in his third year of teaching. He is a talented artist and went into the teaching profession with the same high hopes and expectations as most new teachers. Every month, he calls his parents for a loan to buy food. Stephen cannot believe what he has gotten himself into financially. He is planning to leave teaching. He has decided that if he is going to work that hard, he should be paid accordingly. He listens to the experienced teachers who are still struggling financially after 25 years and does not want to find himself in their shoes 20 years down the road.

Now meet Betty R. Betty teaches 150 students every day. If Betty earned only baby-sitting wages of $3.00 (if you can get a baby-sitter for that these days) for each of her students (per day, not per hour) she would earn $450 per day, or $2,250 per week, or $9,000 per month. Betty is forced to baby-sit some of her students, but she offers them much more should they choose to accept. Although our society will pay a teenager $3.00 OR MORE PER HOUR to baby-sit youngsters, we wouldn't dream of paying that much to educate them! Talk about misplaced American priorities!

If we took the same teacher with the same amount of students and paid her the minimum wage of $5.15 per student, the amount as of this writing, (again not per hour, but per day) she would make $772.50 per day, or $3,862.50 per week, or $15,450 per month.

If we pay her by the hour for each student, seven hours of actual teaching per day (even though teachers work eight hours), the salary would be $5,407.50 per day at minimum wage. **AT MINIMUM WAGE!**

If we pay her baby-sitting wages per hour, per student, for seven hours of actual teaching, she would make $3,150 per day. **AT BABY-SITTING WAGES!**

And with all these amounts, we still wouldn't be paying teachers a red cent for all the over-time they spend in a day!

What! Pay a teacher that kind of money? You have to be out of your mind! That's ridiculous! You can't look at it like that!

Well, why can't you look at it like that? Who says you can't look at it like that? It seems to me, and a few million others in the profession, a teacher should command the same amount of money per hour that a baby-sitter is paid, or a worker who is paid minimum wage. And for those who think that amount of money is too much, go teach school for a week! Teachers more than earn their money! And the next time you hire a baby-sitter, see how much the sitter would charge just to watch 150 or more kids a day and be responsible for them, let alone teach them anything.

How much would day care cost for 150 kids a day?

And go out and find a minimum wage worker and put him/her in charge of 150 people that must be controlled, motivated, taught and their personal problems solved, while stacks of paperwork must also be accurately kept. Do you think you will find anyone to do the job for $5.15 an hour?

Whether we pay our teachers baby-sitting wages or the minimum wage for all their students, these amounts make more sense than what we currently pay them.

"Teachers aren't worth near that much money!" I can just hear the screaming now! I guess it all boils down to where we place our priorities, now doesn't it?

We pay millions of dollars in this country to those who have the skills to throw a large round ball and hit a net with a hole in it.

We pay millions to those who can take a small round ball and hit it with a club, or a racket, or a bat.

And we heap millions and millions of dollars on those who can take an oblong ball and run with it, or fall on it, or kick it, or keep others from getting it.

Entertainers of all kinds and descriptions make millions of dollars because in our culture we love to be entertained by them, and we respect and value those who entertain us.

Our heroes are the athletes, entertainers and stars. Sports and entertainment are just two American priorities.

Here is what one teacher had to say:

"Most people in education are underrated, underpaid, and unappreciated. Until our society begins to value its educators as much as it does our politicians, entertainers and sports figures, I cannot foresee much change. We love to heap our adoration and money on the celebrity and I am sure that gives them all a pretty secure feeling about their self-worth. Meanwhile, we leave our educators to grapple on their own. I am not advocating Emmy Awards Night for educators on television, as I am sure it would be a loser in the Nielsen Ratings, but somehow we must take steps to recognize and reward the tremendous contributions made by teachers." Charlotte I.

Why has there never been any interest in elevating the teaching profession to the level it deserves? Why has it never come close to the law profession or the medical profession in terms of respect and monetary potential? The answer is complex, yet simple...because educators have never demanded it and teachers are not a top American priority. When was the last time you heard about an *influential and powerful* state and federal teacher's lobby? NEVER! And lobbying is the name of the game in the good old USA.

We continue to hear the same sad song about how concerned the federal government is about our educational system. While listening to that concern, we can put men and women into space... we can walk on the moon...we can send thousands of our troops to other countries to fight wars in record time...we can bail out savings and loans...we can either give or lend billions of dollars to foreign countries...and we can witness spending millions upon millions on political campaigns, but we cannot, or will not, provide a public school system that we can point to with pride, or do we care what pay our teachers receive.

Why don't we have an outstanding public educational system throughout this country? Why do we have a major teacher shortage? Because they are not priorities. Important, yes. Priorities, no.

And somebody answer these questions:

Why can't we feed our hungry, or provide affordable health care for our citizens, or care for our elderly? Why is the average working citizen just one or two paychecks away from living on the streets? And why is a non-U. S. citizen able to receive free health care when a citizen and taxpayer cannot? Gads! All these questions are giving me a migraine headache! How about you?

Why is it we can protect other countries, but we cannot provide safe streets and schools in our own country? Why do we close military bases all over America, but we cannot keep inmates in prisons because of overcrowding? And why are some prison inmates receiving Social Security benefits?

And why in heaven's name, did we throw open the borders of Mexico when we spend billions of dollars fighting a hopeless drug war with that same country?

Correct me if I am wrong, but doesn't the federal government operate on taxes paid by the citizens of this nation? If you have taken a class in Government 101, you learned that our government was created **BY THE PEOPLE**, and **FOR THE PEOPLE**. It is OUR GOVERNMENT run with OUR MONEY. Yet, children in America attend schools without enough books or supplies. Kids have insufficient food and clothing. Some children are just plain hungry and the only meal they receive is at school.

Kids spend their days in schools that are so old that they have leaky roofs and classrooms with mold and mildew and roaches large enough to wear flea collars. Many schools are not air-conditioned and some are not heated properly. Meanwhile, back in Washington, our government has spent tax dollars on the effects of cigarette smoking on dogs (what brand does your dog smoke?); the sex life of Japanese quail; the renovation of the House beauty parlor to the tune of $350,000; and the $220,000 some joker authorized to teach college students how to watch television.

We have all heard the stories of government waste...the $100 screws...$500 toilet seats, etc. But my personal favorite is the $19 million plus spent to study whether flatulence emitted by cows and other livestock harms the ozone layer! I didn't read about it, but I wouldn't be surprised if millions were also spent to see if *corks* could be used to solve the problem!

And the hungry should love this one...the $160,000 spent to study food gathering habits of a tribe in Paraguay. Another $50,000 was spent to prove that sheep dogs do, in fact, protect sheep — which has long been a concern of the American people. The search for extraterrestrial life cost $6.1 million and the public wouldn't hear the truth if the results showed we all had an extraterrestrial living next door. That $6.1 million should be a comforting thought for those dying of cancer and with the AIDS virus and other diseases.

Not many years ago forty million dollars was spent to renovate one of the House restaurants in Washington and you can be sure it still doesn't compare to the cuisine and decor of most school cafeterias.

Six million dollars was spent to upgrade the Senate subway system. Aren't school buses good enough for Senators?

Another personal favorite is the $2 million spent to construct and sail an ancient-style canoe to depict the migration of native Hawaiians. Another $49 million was spent for a rock-and-roll museum.

The government we support spent $22 million to find out how long it takes for the mail to be delivered. That one brings tears to the eyes because the answer is: As long as possible, if it gets there at all.

Smokey the Bear's fiftieth anniversary cost the government $200,000 and Smokey is only a figment of our imagination.

The study of "handling animal manure" cost less than $50,000, but is still much more than a school teacher makes in a year. All of these outrageous expenses are only the tip of the bureaucratic iceberg of senseless spending.

Mr. and Ms. Taxpayer already works until noon every day just to pay their share of the present tax bill. Or to put it in another prospective, they work from January until May to pay the taxes that keeps the IRS out of their hair.

The average American citizen who works for a living and pays his/her bills, obeys the law and still believes in the basic principles on which this nation was founded, is **plum taxed out!**

Do we want more of the federal government's big nose in more of our business? Does anyone want the federal government in charge of our public school system? The answer is a loud **NO**! However, if we did not have to fund the federal government's spending incompetence, some of our tax money could remain at the state and local level and be used to better advantage. That's for sure!

Although we constantly read about government waste and see television programs on the subject, what is done about it? What does the average citizen do about it? Nothing! Some of us don't even vote or take an interest in who is sent to Washington to run things, or even who is sent to run things in their own state, for that matter.

And what ever happened to the "checks and balances" system of government? Has government become too big to keep itself in check? What are we going to do about it? What can we do about it? We can vote! We can change laws! We can take back control of our government because it does, after all, *belong to us!*

And one thing is certain...if every taxpayer conducted his/her own spending habits in the same way the government does, the IRS would throw all the taxpayers in jail and the government would fall on its bureaucratic butt!

Will our priorities in America continue down the same old worn path? Will we ever spend as much to educate as we do to eliminate...with the cost of wars and the preparation of wars?

Will we ever feed the hungry in America before we attempt to feed the hungry in the rest of the world?

And two last questions...will we ever spend as much to educate kids as we do to house prisoners...and will we ever pay teachers and provide them with pension benefits with at least as much as we do congressmen and congresswomen?

I wonder...

Do you?

Chapter Fourteen
The Real School House

"...OIS, AIN'T THAT 'THE NERD' FROM HIGH SCHOOL?"

THE REAL SCHOOL HOUSE

Webster's Dictionary defines "school" as a place or institution for education or training. Such a simple and misleading definition.

A school is actually a very strange place. It is a building full of squirming kids of all ages, most of whom really don't want to be there. They are also supposed to be learning things they really don't want to learn.

A school building is furnished with desks and very hard and uncomfortable chairs nobody wants to sit in for very long. There is usually very bad florescent lighting in which nobody can see very well. There is a cafeteria in the school that often serves food that few want to eat and everyone complains about.

There are restrooms with very little or no privacy and more often than not, empty toilet paper and soap dispensers.

There are textbooks that only a very few want to read, some of which even teachers do not like and do not understand who selected or why.

There is a principal in the school house and several vice principals nobody wants to see. There is a superintendent of schools that few do see.

There is a local Board of Education that establishes policies for the school, but doesn't really know what goes on in the school.

The State Board of Education and the State Legislature makes rules and regulations for everyone at the school house to follow. Not only do they not know what goes on there, they have never even been there.

One time, some of these individuals decided that the "open concept" should replace the "self-contained" classroom. So the walls in some schools were knocked down between classrooms. These folks also decided that "team teaching" was the way to go, so teachers were required to learn how to teach in teams. Off the teachers went to school once again.

Well, this open concept was too noisy and didn't work very well, so walls had to be built back and teachers went back to teaching alone. And "team teaching" went by the wayside.

Many things like that have happened in the school house and when they don't work everybody goes back to doing what they did in the first place.

We taught the old math. Then we taught the new math. And now we are going back to teaching the old math.

Reading and spelling was taught phonetically, then it was changed and we taught using the whole word (or memorization) and now the trend is to go back to phonetics.

Another popular trend was Interdisciplinary Thematic Planning, or using one central theme in all classes. If goats happened to be the theme, then all subjects included goats in the curriculum.

Another new term somebody thought up is "higher level critical thinking skills." This is a good idea to have students thinking on a *higher* level. In fact, it is a wonderful idea. But there is one major problem that was overlooked. Teachers are very aware that a large number of students haven't conquered "lower level critical thinking skills" yet. Teachers believe the concept of higher critical thinking skills is like trying to teach someone to run in a marathon...before they have learned to walk. As has been said, it's like "putting the cart before the horse." Nevertheless, teachers were shuffled off to more inservice training and more meetings to hear more than they <u>never</u> wanted to know about higher level critical thinking skills and how to incorporate this into their teaching methods.

Teachers realize that students, for the most part, have not learned the basics they should know. For instance: reading, writing legibly, writing a complete sentence, spelling correctly, adding, subtracting, multiplying and dividing, telling time, and making simple change with money. Few can communicate by putting simple thoughts on paper. Their vocabularies are inadequate because when they were younger they were not read to and now cannot read themselves. And they have not learned to communicate without yelling and using their fists or profanity to get their points across.

In the real school house, teachers spend hour after hour, day after day and week after week trying to get students to merely listen and follow simple directions. They spend their time trying to get students to write complete sentences and write them legibly. They try to get them to spell there/their correctly, or to/too/two, or its/it's and hundreds of more words just like these. And all of this is required before they can attempt to teach their own subjects.

Teachers spend hours trying to get students to grasp the concept that if they don't listen and learn Part A, they won't understand Part B or Part C and on down the line. And if they don't learn during one school year, they will not be able to understand the information in the next school year. Very often, it is a concept students cannot grasp.

Case in point: Sally Porter spent twelve weeks teaching typing on the computer keyboard, all spacing and punctuation rules for typed copy, the functions of word processing and the application of their typing skills, and various word processing activities including reports, math problems, creative writing, restaurant menus, business flyers and the publication of individual newspapers or magazines. The last six week period began with business letters, including all parts of the business letter, as well as three letter forms.

Mrs. Porter went over the information for business letters step by step with the students as they reviewed typed examples while she spoke. She covered the information a second time. Then, she discussed the process a third time using the blackboard.

She explained and explained that *current date* meant *that day.* Three times she explained that an inside address was the *name and address to whom the letter was written and that the same address would appear on the envelope.* In addition, each student had all this in their notebooks. *"Lastly",* Sally Porter said, *"the letter is from you."*

The student's assignment: Type the letter below using the current date and remember the letter is from you. Proof read and use spellcheck before printing.

Sally Porter received: eight typed letters from her students written to themselves with an inside address using their own names and addresses and no closing; five letters typed with the words *current date*; six letters that students had typed *to and from themselves*; and one student signed his letter: *You.*

In addition, while completing sample job applications, more than half her students typed in this blank: Sex YES! **Please, don't talk to Sally Porter about higher level critical thinking skills!**

Teachers in the school house are silent voices by nature, except among themselves. Their opinions have seldom been respected, sought or taken seriously. They aren't encouraged to speak up or to defend what they believe if it differs from central administration or state government. Perhaps, this is because they are thought of as "tall children" or the "hired help" and not professionals or experts in educational processes.

If experienced teachers are not the experts on schools, teaching and learning, who is? Is central administration? Is the local school board? Are college professors? Or is it the governors, state boards and state legislators? Actually, no...none of these individuals are experts. They are not in the trenches.

The expertise that it takes to do all that is required of a teacher and to accomplish all that they do is truly mind boggling. And while they do not have control over their own profession, they still manage to educate millions of young people every year. And the younger and less experienced teacher coming into the classrooms today will not stay as teachers have done in the past. They won't unless public education changes drastically...and very soon.

What is taught in the school house is decided by someone other than teachers. This generally is decided by the rulemakers and policymakers. They decide what is to be taught, how long it will be taught and how it should be taught. A good example of this **is world history**, a required course in high school.

The curriculum begins with 1800 B.C. and *ends with the present year*. This time period involves all countries of the world and includes: their governments, religions, cultures, international relations, revolutions, famous people, geography, wars and its impact on the United States, as well as the new global world in which we live.

In addition, time must be spent on current events, such as the Persian Gulf War and the *coup d' etat* in Russia. These four thousand years must be taught in approximately 175 days...consisting of two semesters minus the days students are out of class for various extracurricular activities. FOUR THOUSAND YEARS IN 175 DAYS OR LESS! In contrast, *two years* are used to cover 200 years of American history.

In today's curriculum, in addition to regular studies, teachers must also spend time teaching drug abuse, law enforcement, teenage pregnancies, AIDS prevention, values clarification, violence intervention, peer pressure, manners and behavior expectations while at the same time counseling those students who have problems they cannot deal with alone. Wouldn't everyone agree it is humanly impossible for teachers to spend their day doing the job fifteen people and fighting an uphill battle all the way?

American public schools have antiquated curriculums. Even though only approximately 18 percent of the population in this country have college educations, our curriculum still tends to focus on the college bound student. At the same time, college tuitions are rising and student loans are decreasing. It is becoming more and more difficult for those students who want to and are qualified to attend college to do so.

From the trenches:

"We do not have enough job related courses. Students who will never see a college campus are still diagramming sentences and struggling through algebra." Brenda B.

"Is the curriculum adequate? You tell me. Students cannot read or spell, add or subtract, or communicate with others. They have no idea what the word responsibility means and they don't care. High school graduates think they will start their first job at $30,000." Samuel E.

"We should eliminate about 50 percent of the "book learning bunk" we throw at students and teach them survival techniques for the work world." Michelle W.

"Somehow we must get across to students that the world does not owe them a living. Students aren't interested in anything other than what they are going to do that night." Peter Q.

Everybody screams that students who are high school graduates cannot hold an entry level job. However, nobody cares about requiring business courses in the curriculum. In fact, every year there are more and more business courses dropped from high school curriculums.

There has never been an attempt to coordinate an educational plan toward anything except receiving the required credits. Subjects that help students in the work world are not emphasized or required. When students graduate, they are not equipped to seek employment. They try to enter the work force with no idea of what they owe their employers in terms of being reliable, on time and at work every day...much less being honest, loyal, compatible with co-workers and giving their employer a day's work for a day's pay.

Somehow, some way, students must be made to understand that if they want anything in this life they must work for it. After all, there is no such thing as a "free lunch." And when students are told all those free breakfast and lunch meals at school are paid for with taxpayer's money, they are astonished. If a teacher would take the time to divide a class into two parts: Part 1 — the hardworking taxpayers, and Part 2 — the unemployed on welfare...then, explain how Part 1 is providing all of these benefits at no cost for Part 2 individuals. Both sides would have learned a valuable lesson. This is all new information for students and something they can identify with on a personal basis.

Young people leave school as dropouts or graduates and know nothing of proper grooming, how to interview for a job, or what an employer is looking for in an employee.

Most students do not know how to handle credit or a personal checking account. And they don't have a clue about the high cost of surviving financially. This certainly explains the vast number of young people still living at home with their parents. They don't know how to manage money, how to be a smart consumer, or the importance of insurance.

We cannot teach everything a student should know in public schools. This will always be an impossibility. Although, there are those who think this should be the school's responsibility. One thing we can do...we *can* teach differently.

At present, there is too much to teach in core subjects. Teaching **THE TEST**, plus all the other distractions already mentioned are additional burdens.

First and foremost, we must offer those students who will not pursue a higher education curriculum choices that will be helpful in their lives. It would be an ideal situation if every student could and would excel in math and science as well as graduate from high school. It would be wonderful if all students could go to college and graduate. But that will not happen.

While I may not be an educational genius, I do possess common sense. And it would be fair to state that nobody has *all* the answers to our educational problems, least of all myself. But there are some solutions that teachers know would make a big difference in changing the direction of public schools...currently headed on a downward spiral very rapidly.

If our goal is to make public schools into high-priced social services agencies and day care centers staffed with people who used to be educators, then we are right on target!

If we are going to make public schools places to focus on the ills of society and to accommodate all the needs of special needs students, at-risk students and the "just gimme a zero" crowd, or force everyone else into charter schools and private schools, then we are headed in the right direction.

But if our goal is to focus on — and adequately educate — those students who want an education, we are way off target!

If our intention is to upgrade the teaching profession, keep experienced teachers and attract the best people to the profession, again, we are continuing in the wrong direction.

Teaching and learning can be relatively simple once again. However, sending students into the classroom who have been up until 2:00 a.m. watching television or working at a job to pay for a car, who have not done their homework or studied for a test, have not eaten since the day before, are habitually late or absent, are disruptive or unresponsive, have parents who never check homework or report cards and do not consider an education as a top priority for their children, then teachers can *guarantee* these students *will not* learn. Teachers can give a full and unconditional guarantee on this point!

We can hold teachers accountable. We can hold principals accountable. And we can yell about THE TEST and continue to scream from the rooftops the phrase, "all children can learn", but these students will be exactly what they have worked to be...uneducated! There are no two ways about it and this is the hard, true lesson of reality.

American students who think an education is a waste of their time, has no purpose or believe it has a purpose, but it is just too much trouble, refuse to see the connection between an education and their future. These students have no goals and are accustomed to circumstances involving instant gratification. Education certainly does not gratify instantly. Some students view the goal oriented and high academic achievement students as "nerds." And they make fun of these students by calling them "school boys and school girls."

Students must be taught that the students they refer to as the "nerds" will become the ones who will drive the nice cars, live in the nice houses, wear the nice clothes and probably become financially successful. These "nerds" will be the backbone of this country and will support this country with tax money they will earn through hard work. These "nerds" will be the voters and the law-abiding citizens who will make it possible for every child in this country to receive an education. These "nerds" will be the ones who pay for medical insurance for their families, care about their credit, and pay their bills. And these "nerds" will be the ones who pay for welfare, county health care, support charitable organizations, maintain police and fire departments and pay for prison systems for the benefit of all society.

Meanwhile across town, those who made fun of the ones called "nerds" in school will become the uneducated and un-skilled poor of this nation. They will contribute little to society, because they didn't believe in the value of an education. They will not have the tools to make their lives better. Until they understand this — at an early age, hopefully — public education doesn't have a chance. Teachers can offer them the tools they need, but that's all they can do.

Parents must reinforce the message to their children that education *must* come before television, sports, jobs, cars and their social life. And the real heroes at school are the ones who succeed in academics... not just in athletics.

EDUCATORS CANNOT SEND THIS MESSAGE ALONE. What educators can do — and what they do best — is give their stu-dents the tools to survive and succeed. Given the proper re-sources, they can educate our young people, but they cannot be expected to be parent, social worker, police officer and teacher at the same time.

The educational system must also put academics and per-formance ahead of all extra-curricular activities. This is what teachers have to say on that subject:

"The classroom takes a back seat to everything else going on in public schools. If administrators say differently, they either aren't telling the truth or aren't smart enough to know the truth. Everything imaginable is going on in schools and it's the classroom that suffers." Barbara K.

"Good teachers, experienced teachers, have quit or are going to quit, because academics is at the bottom of the list and they are tired of fighting it. There was a time when other things went on at school, but they were at the bottom of the list and academics came first." Ester P.

"We are given so much to cover in one year and expected to spend a large part of the day preparing for THE TEST. I always feel

like I'm dancing as fast as I can!" J.M.

"Morale is at an all-time low. Every year we are given more and more responsibility. The negative is emphasized and the millions who receive a good education are not news. Teachers are so fed up and burned out!" Mary H.

"Teaching is more complex and multifaceted than most adults could possibly realize because they are basing their beliefs on school as they knew it." Stephen R.

"I don't know what parents are doing as far as parenting is concerned. They certainly are not teaching the basic social skills, self discipline, respect, manners, or the value of an education. I am thankful for those parents who are caring and helpful toward their children and logical when it comes to dealing with teachers." Larry H.

"In this violent world we live in today, it is ridiculous to believe that schools are safe places. Students are not safe with each other and teachers are not safe with certain students. Wake up America! We are fighting a war in our public schools!" Liz L.

"The real schools of today are not what most people envision. Kids don't care if they receive a zero or how many they receive. Others just want to get by with the easiest way possible. The curriculum revolves around THE TEST. The teachers revolve around trying to do their jobs in classrooms which revolves around everything and everybody except them." Jason M.

"If students can pass a ball, teachers are expected to pass them." Maurine P.

"Schools should put in revolving doors because kids are coming and going all the time during school hours. They are going on field trips, music and band trips and extra-curricular competitions just to mention a few." Lane S.

We have to change the curriculum to meet the needs of today's world. We must do away with at least half of the bureaucratic rubbish that is thrown at teachers, since they simply don't have time for it.

We must, somehow, find people who have some idea of the reality of today's classroom and exercise common sense in making the decisions that govern public education by allowing teachers to run their own show. Otherwise, Webster's Dictionary will have to change the definition of school as "a place or institution that was *formally* used for education or training."

Chapter Fifteen
The Day OurSchool Burned

THE DAY OUR SCHOOL BURNED

To understand this saga, you must walk along with us from the day it all began on that cold December Saturday morning.

Telephones were ringing all over the city with the same horrible news: "Our school is on fire!" And indeed, we could see the smoke bellowing up from miles away. Watching that black smoke climbing toward the sky, we thought we knew how devastating it would be. But we couldn't know the extent of the devastation. Not then.

In your mind's eye, stand with us for the first time as we looked at the burned-out shell of what was once our junior high school. Most of the teachers had been there for years and the school had become a second home of sorts. The members of the faculty had become an extended family to each other. We *were* family...from our principal, the office staff, the teachers and students, to the cafeteria and custodial personnel. We supported and cared for each other with a dedication that can only be described as very special and unique.

The offices of the school and the eighth grade wing of the two story building were gutted. Classrooms were gone. Books and personal effects were now only ashes. All that had been left at school on Friday afternoon was gone forever. And the school cafeteria that was so familiar would not serve another meal.

Most of us had never experienced a fire that affected us on a personal level. We were not prepared for the first glimpse of the destruction and devastation. But how can anyone prepare for the aftermath of a fire?

On that Saturday afternoon as we stood at the site, there was an overwhelming silence and feeling of shock. Next came the feelings of deep sadness and sorrow coupled with a sense of hopelessness. Suddenly, we felt the realization of someone experiencing the emotions of what can best be described as a death. And it *was* like a death because we had lost something that was a big part of our lives that we had taken for granted. Now it was gone.

Miraculously, the two-story seventh grade wing located behind the burned structure remained standing and largely untouched by the fire. The events that followed on that December Saturday to the following Monday morning seem impossible all these years later.

154

Teachers and students did not miss one day of school! All 1800 students and their teachers never skipped a beat! How was that possible?

The impossible became the possible due to the determination, hard work and the fighting spirit of the PTA, parents, students, faculty and staff. These individuals spent Saturday night, Sunday and Sunday night forming a campaign...complete with signs and publicity to BUILD BACK OUR SCHOOL!

School staff hurriedly set up offices in the seventh grade wing. Sack lunches were planned for Monday to feed the masses. A new entrance to the school was quickly formed and the dangers of the burned building section was fenced off.

Plans were quickly made to house eighth grade students and teachers in the seventh grade wing.

Unavoidably, each morning the seventh graders and their teachers would be handed their sack lunches as they boarded buses to travel to and from a nearby junior high school. Understandably, they were not welcomed with open arms at their "new" school. They had suddenly caused severe overcrowding in the host school with all the problems that such a situation creates. Some classes had to be held at the end of hallways when classrooms were full to capacity. It was a long and disappointing year for adults and students alike.

When the burned-out portion of the school was structurally secure, teachers donned hard-hats and in small groups followed our principal into the dark and terrifying belly of the building to look for salvageable personal possessions.

Teachers lost most or all of their books, papers and teaching aids they had spent years collecting. Neither the school district or the teachers had insurance to cover these items.

One small filing cabinet was found with all its contents intact...only burned around the edges and with the odor of fire that remained for years to come. Next to the small filing cabinet was another larger one completely burned to a crisp.

A teacher found the sweater she kept on the back of her desk chair with a large burn on the sleeve. All that remained of the chair was one charred leg. To walk through the remains of a fire is indescribable. There is no rhyme or reason as to what a fire will leave behind.

Teachers began to teach their students Monday morning with very little to teach with....a few shared books and chalk that was in short supply. Giving half a chalk stick to another

155

teacher was common and comical. Often overheard were the words "I'll show you my chalk if you'll show me yours!" Sometimes humor bordered on uncontrollable giddiness. But it helped get us through the days.

Several events stick in the memory of the people who endured that year. However, what stands out is the attitude of the central administration. Not once did the faculty and staff hear the words: "We understand the hardships you are facing and will support and help you in every way we can." Although the central administration *never* really understands what actually goes on in the classroom, we waited for those words of encouragement and support. They never came.

What we did hear was the remark the superintendent of schools made: *"Now we will see who the real teachers are!"*

And the first supplies we received for assistance? Paper clips!

BUILDING BACK

Becoming involved with the power of a fire teaches many lessons to many people. One of the first things learned is to appreciate fully those wonderful professionals called firemen and firewomen. Not only do these men and women save lives and property, they risk their own lives in the process. They witness daily the terrible devastation and destruction that fire can bring. Whatever they are paid for their services isn't nearly enough. To watch them at work is a sobering and humbling experience. They are indeed very special people.

The fire department confirmed what had been suspected. ARSON! How could anyone deliberately set fire to our school? Who would do such a thing?

Three young boys managed to gain entry into the building, make a couple of phone calls in the office area, and then go about their task of setting a fire that would cost millions of dollars and affect the lives of many children and adults for the next three years. Were they punished for their deed? They were juveniles, so what do *you* think?

As we looked out of our second-story classroom windows every day we looked down on the blackened remains of our school and learned very quickly we were witnessing scenes similar to what a war zone must be like. History teachers included this very real scenario in their lesson plans on war. Destruction has its own unique smells, sounds and lessons. And although they will fade from memory, they are never forgotten.

Both students and adults alike learned almost immediately that they had a fighting spirit that would not only get them through the hard times ahead, but would bring them even closer in the process.

Those who had seemed to be humorless before the fire, became humorous after the fire. Those who had been humorous, became more so. Humor managed to brighten the days for everyone — especially those in despair. No matter the ordeal, we found something to laugh about. But one science teacher gave us the way-down-deep belly laugh of that year...

Outside the building workmen continued their task of hauling debris from the fire and preparing to rebuild. Heavy equipment was everywhere...coming and going...lifting and dumping...and knocking down.

Inside the building Mrs. Pipp, *science teacher extraordinaire*, sat at her desk in her classroom on the first floor calmly talking to her students about their homework assignment.

Mrs. Pipp, not one to get overly excited about anything, felt a vibration and heard an unusual noise coming from the wall behind her chair. Suddenly, as a bulldozer plowed through the wall, Mrs. Pipp jumped out of her chair and straight into the air and screamed as loudly as she could, "Son-of-a bitch!" And given the circumstances who could blame her? And nobody did. Her reaction seemed entirely appropriate. *(I still laugh when thinking about it!)*

Bulldozers and wrecking balls began their assault under our watchful eyes. Those of us perched on the second floor watched the wrecking ball swing toward us for days. We sent up silent prayers that the operator knew his job well and had a steady hand. Many a time we heard somebody yell, "Here comes the ball! Hope it doesn't kill us all!"

When it rained, we watched rats diving in and out of standing water. The rubble became larger and larger. The war zone became more pronounced. Would it all ever end?

Finally, the time came when the rubble disappeared and the girders for the new building came into view. Progress at last.

One especially fine spring day Mr. Lock, history teacher and one of the most humorous people on earth, came walking into my classroom with a look of amazement. Walking over to my desk he leaned down and said in a very low voice, "Tell me, does Wally Workman there have on the proper attire?"

Glancing out my window, I gasped as my mouth flew open..and thirty eighth grader's eyes immediately looked up and toward the window to see what had made their teacher gasp.

Not a foot away, perched on a girder, was a workman complete with hard-hat and munching on a sandwich without a care in the world. The T-shirt he wore sported bright red lettering with the message: **HAPPINESS IS A TIGHT PU—Y!**

What to do? What to do? The students were mumbling among themselves and some were asking each other, "What does that mean? What does that mean?"

Mr. Lock was wringing his hands, while I on the other hand began writing the following note to the principal who had quite a sense of humor himself:

Red alert! Red alert! Suggest you pop on your hard-hat and climb up the girder to the one just outside our windows. Mr. Lock and I do believe this would come under the description of CLASS DISTURBANCE! BIG TIME CLASS DISTURBANCE!

In a matter of minutes we saw the workman climb down from his perch...only to reappear a few minutes later with the addition of masking tape on his shirt. Now the shirt read: **HAP-PINESS IS.**

One last item on this subject...Mr. Lock made a sign for one of the female history teachers who was unaware of the spectacle on the second floor. He told her we were all going to wear the same sign. After hanging one around her neck, he sent her to the principal to show off our new signs. Her sign read: **HERE COMES HAPPINESS!**

We all had a laugh — including our principal — at the expense of the unsuspecting teacher who turned beet red when hearing the real story. She couldn't get her sign off fast enough!

There are many stories from this time of rebuilding. Stories of humorous happenings....stories of frustration and helplessness...stories of sadness...and stories of self-examination and lessons learned.

Eventually, the school was rebuilt. Now we had new classrooms with new furniture and equipment to replace the old. We had carpet on the floors for the first time. Female teachers enjoyed the new desks that didn't snag their hose as the old ones had. Chalk was plentiful and everyone had a book. And best of all...no more sack lunches. All the students and teachers were together again in one school. And it must be said that the group of people who made up that particular faculty and staff were the best that could be found anywhere. They were loyal, hard-working and determined to give their best to the students and to each other. We indeed found out who the *real teachers* were. They *all* were!

We gained a wonderful new school, but we lost something, too. Even today, many years later, conversations of reminiscing about the past are always preceded by, "It was before the school burned." It was a marker in all of our lives. And those who were there will never forget the December Saturday morning when the "family" pulled together as one.

Chapter Sixteen
School Daze

ɔK, TEACHERS! READY YOURSELVES FOR FIRST PERIOD!"

SCHOOL DAZE

THIRD PERIOD

Mrs. Porter rushed to her mailbox in the office before third period and found another handful of papers. *Great! More paper-work,* she thought as she headed for the restroom. If she was late to class, so be it. Breathing a sigh of relief when she found the women's bathroom was all hers, she opened the door and locked it behind her.

As the tardy bell rang, Mrs. Porter ran out of the restroom at breakneck speed. Somewhere behind her she heard a voice yelling, "Hold it, Sally! Your skirt is caught up in your pantyhose and I can see your rear-end!" Embarrassed as she felt behind her, Mrs. Porter began to pull and tug everything back into place. She thanked Betty Green and offered up a silent thanks that Betty had been the one to see the spectacle and not her students. What a riot that would have created!

Mrs. Porter's third period is one of her better classes...with only two behavior problems. The majority of the students are hard working and well behaved...25 students in all. However, the two behavior problems are a handful to manage.

Jose is in her class for the second time, repeating the eighth grade this year. He has not matured since last year, and is performing much as he did then...very little academically and a great deal socially. He spends a lot of time outside the door in the hallway because he disrupts the rest of the class. His present average is 31. He is lazy and uncooperative and a member of a local gang. He will be passed on next year even if he fails again, thereby becoming a problem for someone else. Or he may drop out of school if he isn't shot by a gang member first. Jose will not learn anything. Jose refuses to learn anything.

Jack is another problem. He must be handled with kid gloves because he is subject to outbursts that can result in a crisis situation. Mrs. Porter is never very comfortable around Jack, but nobody cares if she is comfortable or not. The students are afraid of Jack. Nobody cares about that either. Jack cannot be denied an education.

If Jack isn't in the mood to work or maybe mad at some-body or some thing, he becomes extremely difficult to manage. He is accustomed to doing what he wants...when he wants. Luckily, he has not had any serious outbursts in Mrs. Porter's classroom, but the crisis intervention techniques for Jack and all the other students with behavior disorders are taken very seriously by teachers. These techniques include:

- Never grab or touch a violent student unless he is harming himself or another person.
- Send for help.
- Keep a normal distance from the student.
- Keep your voice normal and remain calm.

Of course, if a student becomes violent with another student, it is up to the teacher to take care of the situation before helps arrives. Jack is twice as big as Sally Porter and that fact is never far from her thoughts. She really doesn't think this type of student belongs in the public school system. She also wonders if it is time for teachers to wear protective combat gear to class.

Five of her students have special modifications, but work well in class. Mrs. Porter explains the lesson and asks the class to get to work. As she walks around the room, she notices that all students are working with intense concentration at the computers. *It's a lovely day in Mrs. Porter's neighborhood,* she silently sings to herself as she watches her students.

Not so fast, Sally Porter! The fire bell clangs its loud blare and Mrs. Porter hurriedly gets the students out of her classroom, down the hall and out the nearest exit. There had been no time to grab her coat and the cold wind whipped her skirt up and around her legs. *I should have left my skirt tucked into my pantyhose after all,* she laughingly thought to herself. When the all-clear bell rings and 1,200 junior high students begin their return to classes, it closely resembles the invasion of Normandy!

Rest assured, if anything happens out of the ordinary during a school day — including fire drills — students absorb some sort of strange chemical from outer space that seems to make them loud, screaming, punching, hyperactive lunatics. The other types of events that induce this behavior would include pep rallies, assemblies and bomb threats. Precious few will go back to class and resume any type of calm behavior after these experiences.

Invariably, schools have the strange notion that the time to have fire drills, pep rallies, or other activities, is at the beginning of class periods just when students have settled down after

163

change of classes. Is there ever a good time to throw hundreds of students together?

Today is no exception. Mrs. Porter herds her students back into the room and quickly notices that five are missing. She manages to get some degree of order and most of the students resume typing at their computers.

Sticking her head out of the door, Sally looks up and down the hall for her missing students. She sees Jack being escorted down the hall by the police officer and a vice principal...closely followed by Jose with a bloody nose being attended to by the school nurse. Minutes later, Sally receives a note from the office informing her that the three remaining students — all girls — have been found in the restroom smoking. All five students will be sent to in-school suspension or alternative school, *if* there is room for them. Fighting and smoking are against the rules...today. More paper work will be required by Mrs. Porter as a result of these incidents. She also must prepare extra assignments for each student for each day they will be out of her class. When they return to class they will, of course, be behind.

As the bell rings ending the period, Mrs. Porter is glad to have her 45-minute conference and planning period coming next. Hopefully, she will have a chance to catch up on some paperwork and have a few minutes to catch her breath.

FOURTH PERIOD

Sally Porter swallows two big gulps of her soft drink, sits down at her desk and grits her teeth as she gets out her "TO DO" list.

But first, she looks over a "Contract and Bonus" program sent by the counselor and resident police officer for at-risk students. This program was developed by the local police department.

She has been sent seven contracts for seven of her students. All of these students are failing and are behavior problems. The program is designed to motivate these students — **with money** — to sign contracts and do the following for a specific amount of time:

- Attend school regularly. *(Never mind that this is the law.)*
- Arrive both at school and to classes on time.
- Not to disturb classes.
- Complete and turn in assignments.

- Bring books and supplies to class.
- Stay out of fights and the office for school offenses.
- Receive tutoring from teachers if needed.
- Have a library book during reading time.
- Keep notebook in order.
- Wear eye glasses if applicable.

Each contract is worth $15.00 if honored and a student may have as many as four contracts at one time. No student can, however, earn more than $60.00 per month.

These kids are receiving money to do what they are supposed to do and expected to do, Sally thought. *Here we are, sending the wrong message again. When and if they ever get a job, I am sure they think they will get a bonus if they go to work regularly, get their work done, stay out of fights with co-workers and don't get sent to the boss for bloodying somebody's nose. We certainly don't pay the kids money who work hard and do what they are suppose to do. We pay the ones who don't. What a program! Shut-up Sally...nobody cares what you think!*

In the Contract and Bonus program, Mrs. Porter must give her input on each student and address what is needed from the students in her class. She must write her comments and keep up with the progress of each contract. More paper work for teachers.

Sally Porter looks at her "TO DO" list and feels her neck muscles tighten and the beginning of a bad headache. The immediate items requiring attention are:

- Administrative memos regarding: Student Council election, citizenship grades determined by disciplinary slips, flu shots for teachers, ideas to increase attendance, attendance rolls, Kindness Week ideas, drug survey. *(Lot of paperwork here!)*

- Assignments for in-school suspension and alternative school with 12 to be completed...including the five students to be sent today. *(A lot more paperwork added to the pile.)*

- Grade six sets of student papers...the never ending paperwork.

- Get student handouts for classes ready and printed for next week. *(Plenty of paperwork.)*

165

- Complete an in-service survey. (Boring paperwork.)

- Read new modifications for eight students.

- Highlight the names of 50 of her students on a list attending a field trip on Thursday who must not be counted absent on class rolls.

- Complete eight special education reports for students who failed last six weeks. *(More paperwork requiring immediate attention.)*

- Write six passes for students to come to sixth period study class to make up work.

- Complete progress reports for three week period. (Paperwork galore.)

- Type a test for Friday and have it printed.

- Select a "student of the week" for next week.

- Nominate a "teacher of the year."

- Vote on a faculty member for the sick bank committee.

- Develop and type two math worksheets and presentations to assist a first year teacher who is having a rough time.

- Type a documentation for a student from last semester giving the reasons for his failure. The parents' finally want to know why their kid failed the course. *(At least 30 minutes of paperwork.)*

- Make lesson plans for next week...stating objectives, resources used, activities planned and how students will be evaluated. Send copy to the office.

- Complete a budget request for items needed for next year. *(Due Friday.)*

- Complete reports for four students in special education. (Constant paperwork.)

- Enter 165 students' grades into the computer which consists of ten grades per student...1,650 grades total. Remove withdrawn students' names and add new students' names.

- Check 30 computers and printers for keys missing and other problems. Clean all computers. Call repair service if needed.

- Room needs dusting; desks cleaned; files put away.

Sally finished the list, sat back in her chair and closed her eyes. *HOW am I going to get all this done? WHEN am I going to get all this done? WHY do I have to get all this done?*

Reaching into her purse, she fished around for something for her headache. She swallows two pills and leaned her head back against her chair. Closing her eyes again, she began to think about her life and all the days, weeks, months and years she had spent teaching kids. What had it all really meant? Had she made a difference? Sure, her students had come back to see her over the years. She always asked the same question, "Did you learn anything in my class? Have you used that knowledge in school and in your job?" Most said they had. Some said they hadn't tried to learn back then and they were sorry now. She was now teaching the children of former students.

Through the years, Sally had made wonderful friends among the faculty. And there had been some rewards of satisfaction with some of her students. But as the years passed, teaching had become an enormous jagged mountain to climb. It was an everyday struggle with frustrations, disappointments and feelings of ineffectiveness and dissatisfaction. And the mountain had gotten larger and more difficult with each passing year.

I would have to describe it as being able to do much less teaching and doing more dodging of boulders that students and the bureaucracy keep throwing off the top of that mountain, Sally thought. *And I'm always standing knee-deep in paperwork. Then, of course, there is the money. I will never be able to live on my retirement, no matter how long I continue to teach.*

Sally, like thousands of teachers who are heads of their household, had no investments and no savings account. She had raised two children alone — barely getting by and living from paycheck to paycheck. Even now, with her children grown, it still took every penny just to pay bills. And she couldn't play

167

catch-up. She drove a fourteen year old car, never took vacations and bought fewer clothes than anyone she knew. She ate out with friends very seldom. She was paying the mortgage and upkeep on the home her mother had so graciously made the down payment on.

It seemed to Sally that after 28 years of teaching school she should at least have some money in the bank or an investment or two. But where would it come from? There were many times when her kids were young that she didn't know if the food would last until the next monthly paycheck. But somehow, she had always made it from one month to the next. She was still doing the very same thing after all these years...trying to make it from one paycheck to the next.

Each small pay increase was usually followed by larger increases in taxes, telephone, utility and insurance premium cost. One step forward...five steps backward.

Is this a profession or just a low paying thankless job? Sally had asked herself that question many times. *Face it Sally, you know the answer so quit bitching about it! No! Something should be done about it!*

How many times had Sally Porter heard that tired old cliché: "If teachers wanted to make money, they should never have gone into teaching. Teachers should be dedicated to their jobs."

Well I'm tired of the word dedication and I'd like to know if anybody has ever eaten a big plate of dedication? Has anyone ever paid a bill with dedication? Has anyone ever been able to save large amounts of dedication or invested dedication? And after a lifetime of educating thousands of kids, has anyone ever been able to retire comfortably on dedication?

Sally opened her eyes, smiled to herself and realized her head had stopped hurting. As she leaned forward over her desk to begin working, the bell rang. *My whole conference period is gone! It's time for my next class and I didn't get anything done. I still have four more classes, it's still Monday, I still have all this work to do and my head hurts again! Hang on, Sally...you can do it!*

FIFTH PERIOD

Sally's fifth period class begins at 11:35 a.m. and ends at 1:00 p.m. From 11:35 until 12:05, students go to the cafeteria for lunch, so actual class time is 60 minutes. There are 29 students in the class and Sally expects them to complete more work than the other classes who meet for only 45 minutes.

Sally Porter is lucky this semester because she has a great fifth period class. Last semester, half of her fifth period class seemed to be in training to be terrorists while the other half appeared to be in a coma.

The name of the game for fifth period is keeping students busy from the minute they walk into the room until the minute they walk out.

While her students were in the cafeteria, Sally ate her sandwich she had brought from home, ran to the bathroom, checked to see that her skirt wasn't stuffed in her pantyhose, unlocked her classroom door and locked up her purse.

There were no serious behavior problems in this class, but a few of her students would try the patience of the Lord if He came to visit. Members of the class began to wander in from lunch one at a time. Some were hyperactive... acting as if they had just left an exciting football game... while others were lethargic...barely able to put one foot in front of the other. After calling roll, Sally explained the assignments and the class was soon working quietly.

There was one computer in front of Mrs. Porter's desk that often made her remember. That was where Raye sat. Sally had seen some terrible things during her years of teaching, but Raye had remained in her mind and heart.

Raye was a thin and frail young girl. Her clothes were old and faded, but clean. She sat at the computer directly in front of Sally's desk, eyes usually downcast, and she never seemed to smile even when Sally thought she had said something funny enough to be on television. She had wondered many times what the story with Raye might be and had looked for bruises or marks on her arms and legs when she would walk past her desk. She made a point of talking to Raye each day and eventually Raye responded.

Raye learned to type and was proud of her new skills. To actually see the results of learning and accomplishment, coupled with the self esteem it can bring, is one of the perks of teaching computers.

Sally had worried about what would happen when the weather turned cold, because she had never seen Raye with a sweater or coat on chilly days. In her mind, Sally had planned how she would go about getting Raye a coat without hurting her feelings or her dignity.

One day, Sally noticed something different about Raye.

She kept her head down, had nothing to say to Sally and seemed to be in a world of her own. As Sally walked by Raye's desk, she patted her on the back and asked her if anything was wrong. As Sally watched, big tears began to roll down Raye's face before she could put both hands up to hide. "Let me help you Raye," Sally whispered, as she bent over so nobody else could hear. "You can't help me. Nobody in this world can help me," she cried through her hands.

Sally helped Raye out of the room and down the hall to the counselor's office. The events of the next few weeks made Sally Porter heartsick.

Raye, interviewed by the counselor, told how she had been sexually molested by her father and photographed during the act by a friend of her father. The counselor notified Child Protective Services who came and picked her up from school. Raye was removed from the home. The police were called, the father was arrested and charges were filed.

Raye told how her father had molested her for several years and how he had photographed the sexual molestation and sold the photos for profit. Two younger boys still lived in the home, but according to Raye, they had not been sexually abused.

The father was released on bail and had been ordered out of the home. Raye moved back home with her mother and brothers. Was there a happy ending? Hardly.

All photographs had mysteriously disappeared from under the bed where her father had kept them. It would be Raye's word against her fathers.

Soon after Raye was allowed to move back home, her mother had a little talk with Raye in her tiny bedroom on the back of the old and cluttered house they called home. Raye's mother told her that if she didn't drop the charges and refuse to testify against her father, Raye and her two little brothers and her mother would have to move out on the streets and they would all starve to death. They needed her father to support them, she told Raye. And it would be all Raye's fault if they starved to death. What a heavy burden to put on a 13 year-old girl. Raye confided this information to her best friend who later told the school counselor.

Daddy dearest never went to court. The charges were dropped for lack of evidence and Raye's refusal to testify. Raye never came back to school and the family moved away soon after Daddy came home to his family. And Raye was right...nobody could help her.

Sally Porter often wondered what finally happened to Raye and if there isn't a special place God has picked out for all child sex abusers when they die. And, hopefully, unique accommodations for the mothers of those children who knew it was going on in the home, but did nothing to protect their children.

Sally's thoughts came back to the present and her class. Everyone was working on their quiz assignment with the exception of Ryan.

"What are you doing, Ryan?" asked Mrs. Porter standing over his desk. "Taking a little nap!" Ryan replied. "Ryan, do you see anything written on the board concerning today's lesson about napping? I'm almost certain I didn't include a nap in the lesson!" Sally said. Ryan slowly raised his head and looked up at Sally Porter. "Have a heart, Mrs. Porter. I didn't get enough sleep last night and none of my other teachers would let me sleep either!" Sally looked at Ryan with gritted teeth and raised eyebrows as she said very softly, "Ryan dear, I will give you exactly one split second to sit up, get your lesson underway and not give me one more ounce of trouble. Is that perfectly clear?" Reluctantly, Ryan did as he was told. Perhaps he might get in a snooze or two next period.

Experienced teachers have a special radar that gives off signals that he/she means business and can usually control discipline without raising their voice. Of course, there are some students who have no built-in radar detectors and either don't know when to back off or don't care. If all students had working radar detectors there would be fewer behavior problems.

The next problem came from Lewis. Sally thought that Lewis often laid awake at night thinking of ways to disturb others, dally around with his work and defy his teachers. . Lewis had no radar detector and wouldn't have used it if he did. Sally was so tired of baby-sitting Lewis and often prayed that his parents would move far away...but so far no luck.

Now, Lewis was standing beside Sally's desk with his quiz in his hand and glancing down at the answer key to the quiz on her desk. "Gee Lewis, I don't believe you're supposed to stand here looking at my answer key while I am busy helping another student" Sally said. "I wasn't looking at your key!" Lewis yelled at the top of his voice. "That's just B.S.!" he announced.

Sally, keeping her cool but wanting to stuff Lewis in the wastepaper basket head first, wrote out a referral form for Lewis to go to the office. "Lewis, do you talk to your mother like that?" Sally asked as she wrote. Lewis glared at her with his best *go to hell* look and replied, "NO!" "Why would you think you could talk to a teacher like that?" Sally asked. Lewis had nothing more to say as he stomped out of the room mumbling under his breath.

Sally never failed to be shocked at what comes out of the mouths of young people. It hadn't been too long ago that a female student had called Sally a "damn f—ing bitch." When she returned to class after two weeks in alternative school, Sally said to her in a private conversation, "You called me a bitch and I'm going to show you what a fantastic one I can be." And she was...no restroom visits, no visits to the water fountain, no privileges and very little personal attention. (Believe it or not, this student responded to the treatment by working hard with great behavior.)

Students should never be allowed to talk to a teacher disrespectfully and allowed to return to class. Over the years, Sally had seen students get away with everything short of murder. And now everybody asks why students act the way they do. They act the way they do because they are allowed get by with it. There are no serious consequences for their behavior and they do not have to take responsibility for their actions. Alternative school visits inspire few students. Detention impresses even fewer.

Our bureaucratic society has invented too many loopholes for the acceptance of unacceptable behavior of students.

These loopholes consist of everything from learning disabilities...to home environment...to miles of red tape involved in the process of removing a student from the classroom...to fear of lawsuits by the school district...to the fact that an education is considered a *right* and not a privilege.

As Sally walked around the room, Mary Jane raised her hand and said, "Mrs. Porter, I just want you to know that instead of having my nails done last night, I canceled my appointment and stayed at home and studied for the quiz!" *That's the 90's for you,* Sally thought to herself.

As class ended, Sally announced a major test for Friday and found two more pills for her throbbing headache. Looking at her hands revealed her nails also needed a coat of polish.

SIXTH PERIOD

Sixth period is a study class where students are supposed to get extra help from teachers, do their homework and study or read. Some of Sally's students use their time wisely and others don't. A few students think of this period as a social time and others as a time to take a nap. Sally runs a tight ship, but she cannot take her eyes off of the crew for a second. She has 22 students during this period, but has had as many as 28 at various times. When some of her own students come in for make-up work, she sometimes has 30 students in the room.

The largest problem with this period is having the same students come to class with nothing to do. These are the students who are failing their classes and are consistently in trouble for their behavior.

Today, she has already moved one student for shooting spit-wads and lost her patience with another student who seemed to think he could talk out loud when he felt the urge. Sally is tired of baby-sitting students and especially those who are repeaters, troublemakers and those who need serious attitude adjustments.

Sally's patience is low, her frustration is high and her desire to continue any association with this type of student is zero. Sally knows that if something isn't done very soon, public schools will be full of only the "I don't want to" and "I don't have to and you can't make me" students. The rest of the group will be in charter or private schools.

SEVENTH PERIOD

Sally has two more classes before her teaching day will end. She is tired and stressed, aggravated and discouraged, but she keeps a smile on her face. The back of her neck hurts and her head feels like it is in a vice. There are seven more days until payday and she has $3.00 in her purse and $12.00 in her bank account. A month is a long time between paydays.

As Sally Porter closed the door behind her, her eyes quickly swept over her seventh period class. She called this class her *class from hell.* She knew only a sadistic computer with a vendetta against her could have put all these kids into one class together.

Preparing to call role, Sally saw Elbert throw his pencil across the room, aiming at and hitting one of Martha Lou's 34-D cups. "Elbert, move up here by my desk and behave yourself.

You know better than to throw anything in class. Have you forgotten about the student who was hit in the eye and had to have surgery?" Sally said.

Elbert, who thought of himself as the school stud, pulled himself up out of his chair and swaggered to the front of the room where he proceeded to stretch out on the floor in the centerfold position. He wore a pair of faddish and faded jeans with large holes in the knees and ragged legs. When told to get up and sit at a desk, he swung his legs around to sit up and shared a horrific sight not only with Sally Porter, but with the entire class as well.

It seems Elbert had worn no underwear to school and there appeared to be two large holes in the crouch of his pants. Out of those holes fell two rounded manly objects in all their glory! Sally's eyes stared at the sight in disbelief...her eyes frozen to the spot...and she couldn't seem to move them to the right or to the left. The class went completely to pieces...laughing...screaming...and then clapping their hands, while Elbert's face turned tomato red.

It was fifteen minutes before Sally had everybody calmed down and quiet. Elbert was sent to the office for improper wearing apparel and class disturbance. *This would make a great argument for school uniforms, Sally laughingly thought to herself.*

As Sally attempted to explain the lesson, George began rocking in his chair back and forth, back and forth, as he often did; Marvin was clicking the top of his ball-point pen, *click, click, click;* and Marcus had pulled his jacket over his head for who knows what reason. Peter was in a serious discussion with Amanda, and the hyperactive champion, Barney, had discovered his chair legs would squeak...so he was squeaking all four legs with a satisfied look of accomplishment on his face. *Squeak, squeak, squeak.*

With her teeth gritted and eyes blazing, Sally announced: "Class, I want complete silence in this room! If a pen drops next door, I want to be able to hear it! Is that clear?"

The 25 students in this class had 96 combined absences last six weeks. Cheating in the class was rampant. There were six failures, five near-failures, eight C's, four B-'s and two A's last six weeks. There were eight 504's (all repeaters), three 03's (special education) and four non-English speaking. One non-English speaking student was extremely hyperactive and slow.

One student was currently in alternative school for telling

a vice principal he was going to "smack her" but he would be returning to class soon. The remaining nine students were a mixture of below average, average and above average.

Another student, Mattie, had such a loud shrill voice that it could probably break glass. When she laughed or screamed or talked loudly, Sally was always afraid her own eardrums would explode making her spend the rest of her life reading lips. Mattie's voice was so irritating that Sally hoped for a nice case of laryngitis for Mattie and a few days of silence. Sally's ears were still vibrating from Mattie's voice during Elbert's earlier fiasco.

Sally managed to get the class under control and to work when the door opened. There stood Alberto J., a new student.

"Hello Alberto." Sally greeted him. "Where have you been going to school all year?"

"I ain't been in school." he said. "I've been in jail for carrying a loaded gun and the judge put me on probation if I went back to school. But he didn't know about the other gun in my trunk. I wouldn't be here if I didn't have to be and I don't know 'nuthin about computers." Alberto informed Sally.

Well isn't this wonderful? I would just love to sit down with that judge and ask him just what in the hell he proposes I do with this boy for the next six weeks of school. He can't type, he knows nothing about computers and school is the last place he wants to be. And, of course, that sadistic computer put him in the **class from hell***. Now how does it go? Life is a bowl of cherries...my glass is half full...I must make lemonade out of lemons and don't forget,* **all kids can learn!** *In the meantime, how I would love to get my hands on that judge!*

Every day brought a new mystery to the *class from hell*. What new problems would have to be solved? What would the new frustrations and aggravations be? What new stunt would a student pull? Seventh period always seemed to drain every ounce of energy from Sally's body. She once told a friend that after seventh period her body felt like it had been run over by a freight train. Today was no different. She could almost feel the train wheels on her back. Sally was delighted when the bell rang to end the period. Only one more class. But it was still only Monday.

EIGHTH PERIOD

The last period of the day! Sally rushed to the faculty restroom, threw cold water on her face, patted it dry and dashed

175

back to her classroom. Eighth period could go either way. The class could be delightful or it could be a pain in the lower posterior. Both students and teachers were tired and stressed by the last period of the day.

The 28 students Sally Porter ended her day with usually worked hard, but like most classes there were three or four students that could ruin the rest of the class.

Big John was one of those students, but he was disruptive in a different sort of way. He always had an ailment. This was his hobby. The only thing Sally hadn't heard him complain about was that his teeth itched! He either had a headache, or his eyes hurt, or his stomach hurt, or he had sprained an ankle or finger, or he had broken his little toe, or his throat was closing up and he was choking to death or he was dizzy. Once, Big John even announced he had PMS. Big John enjoyed poor health, but he didn't enjoy working. Today, Big John is absent. Perhaps he had started his monthly period, or thought he had.

The last time he was absent his mother wrote this note: **Big John was absent from school yesterday because I couldn't get anybody to jump me.** *(His teachers assumed that his mother meant her car.)*

Martin is sixteen, looks twenty, and sports a mustache. Why he is in school is anybody's guess. He has failed more than once and will do so again, but he is too old to remain in junior high school another year. He has been in trouble with the police more than once and he is frequently absent. When he does attend school, he sits at his desk and does nothing. And he doesn't even bother to make it appear that he is busy. He disturbs others sometimes, but mostly he sits at his desk and does nothing. He is old beyond his years and has probably seen many things in his young life. Sally Porter, like most teachers, can often spot the students they believe will likely end up jobless, hopeless and ultimately in prison. Martin is one of those students. But he refuses to change his direction.

Allen is the biggest problem in the class. He is small, hyperactive, very slow academically and he is a Dennis the Menace clone. Allen is into everything... including the trash. He seems to bounce off the walls and off the other students. His black hair is always in his eyes and his nose is always running. Today, Allen has his head on his desk and he is sound asleep. He has exerted great amounts of energy since early morning and he must now recharge himself. Allen usually arrives in

Sally's class already recharged and she uses her last drop of energy to try and contain him. Perhaps, she just will let him sleep. He can't read, seldom does any work and isn't capable of doing much. Sally has worked with Allen many times trying to help him learn, but to no avail. He keeps the class in a constant state of turmoil. Today, Sally has already used her last drop of energy, so she pretends she doesn't know Allen is asleep. She hopes he recharges himself into a real dynamo so that by the time he reaches home Momo and Popo will have to cope with the hyperactivity Sally copes with every day.

Last, but certainly not least, is Wesley. He is in not described in any book yet written on child development. And if he was described as an example in a class of future teachers, they would think he was a figment of somebody's imagination. "You made him up!" they would say. But they would be wrong. Wesley is one of those students a teacher never forgets. And Sally has him the last period of the day.

Wesley is uncontrollable. During the last few years, on the day before a holiday, Wesley has become violent and once even broke another kid's arm. His violence is always consistent with impending holidays. Was this a new disease — Holiday Syndrome? Nobody knew. But Wesley was no longer allowed to attend school on the day before a holiday, because the administration is afraid he will eventually kill someone.

He is severely hyperactive. His mother refuses to put him on medication, even though it is doubtful there is a pill anywhere on earth that can tame Wesley. He loves to yell the "F" word at everybody including his teachers. His dad is in prison and Wesley has been arrested for arson. His latest escapade was putting a box of condoms on a teacher's desk. When the condoms were ignored by his teacher, he finally mentioned them himself. "How did you like the gift I brought you. I hope they fit!" he told his teacher.

Sally hasn't had much trouble with Wesley, but she can't get him to pay attention or follow simple directions. He has never been rude to her, but she never knows when he will yell the "F" word at her. And heaven only knows what else he might decide to do. Just being in the same room with him was stressful.

Today was a relatively good day in eighth period. Most of the students worked well at the computers and completed their lesson. Of course, Allen — asleep at his desk — had something to do with the calm atmosphere, Sally figured. She felt like she couldn't cope with one more thing today. Perhaps the students sensed that. Whatever the reason, the bell finally rang and Sally Porter breathed a sigh of relief.

As Sally closed and locked her door for the day, she flung her purse over one arm and her full tote-bag of paperwork over the other. Starting out the front door she ran into her close friend, Ellen.

"Did you have the kind of day I had?" Ellen asked. Neither Sally or Ellen had any makeup left on their faces. Although Sally's hair was sticking straight up, as if she had had her finger in an electrical socket, Ellen's hair was limp and hanging in her face. They would look great on a recruiting poster titled: **TEACHERS LEAVING THE TRENCHES!**

"Well, let me put it to you this way," Sally answered quietly. "I have been locked up with 184 eighth graders all day and trying to cope with their 184 different personalities as I attempted to teach. And the operative word here is *attempted.* Half of them are orbiting the planet and some are in a coma. I have had to look at a student's testicles...I have been temporarily deafened by a student's shrieks...I have left the restroom with my skirt tucked into my pantyhose...I have had a student tell me that what I said was B.S....I have a new student who is on parole and has a fascination for loaded guns and knows nothing about computers...I have enough paper work to keep not only five people busy, but also enough to choke a horse...it's only Monday and I have $15 between me and poverty. I think my neck is broken...I'm not sure I don't have a stress-induced brain tumor and if I could afford to have an ambulance drive me home I would call for one. Then, I would get under my bed in the fetal position and suck my thumb. What kind of day does it sound like I've had to you?

"Now, Ellen, tell about your day!"

I wrote this poem after I analyzed one of my hectic days in the class-room. It's all true, only the names have been changed.

I FELT GREAT WHEN I CAME TO SCHOOL TODAY!

I felt great when I came to school today!
Until I was told to "go to hell" by my student, Jose.
A gang member sat at his computer in my first period class,
And wrote in indelible ink, KISS MY ASS!
Half of the class didn't study for the test.
They went to a late night concert and didn't get any rest.
Margie got in trouble for wearing short shorts to school.
She told me the vice principal was "just a damn fool."
Bert got up out of his seat, fell and embarrassed himself
        falling over Oliver's feet.
Bert got mad and hit Oliver in the head,
"I'll beat the shit out of you after school!" he said.
Laura had tears running down her face.
Six girls had beat her up because of her race.
Billy's parents are divorcing and he's very sad.
They screamed and yelled all night and his Dad left mad.
Some boys made fun of Jim's clothes and made him cry.
He said to me, "Sometimes I just want to die."
Should I cry, scream, be mad, or be sad...I just can't say.
But I felt great when I came to school today!

Chapter Seventeen
Educational Hopscotch

"OK SENATOR, CALL IT!
HEADS TEACHERS GET A $500 RAISE
... *TAILS* THEY GET NUTHIN'!"

EDUCATIONAL HOPSCOTCH

Is there *anything* great about being a teacher anymore? You bet there is!

There is nothing to compare to that first day of school when all the new faces arrive in your classroom who become **your students.** They are your responsibility. And what an awesome responsibility it is to try and teach them what they should know.

These young faces are apprehensive and worried and excited all at the same time. No matter how old they are, they are still kids...with fears and feelings of inadequacy and also with feelings of expectations. And a teacher's first responsibility is to make each one feel that they are respected and they are special. At the same time, they must understand immediately that they are there to learn and the teacher is in charge. First impressions *are* lasting impressions!

It is both exciting and challenging to discover each very unique personality. Some kids are painfully shy and communication with them is on a quiet one-to-one basis only. The extrovert will communicate anytime and anywhere on any subject. The trick is to make everyone feel equal.

To see a student learn what you have taught him/her is an indescribable feeling of delight. This creates a bond with another human being that is indeed special. It is what being a teacher is all about. There are still many wonderful students who have kept teachers in the classroom trying to do the job they are there to do.

There are all the wonderful surprises that invariably occur on the first day of school. A smart teacher learns very quickly not to judge a student's ability or inability on their appearance, actions or what might have been heard from someone else. A preconceived judgment will often prove you wrong.

The over-sized eighth grade boy who says very little, doesn't smile and appears to be day dreaming, turns out to be the one who learns quickly and has a talent for creative writing that is astonishing. And when you tell him how proud you are of him and how impressed you are with his talent, his chest expands, he stands taller for the first time as he responds with a smile you have not seen before. This student will remember those words of praise and encouragement long after you have forgotten him. For the time you have him in class, he will become a different student altogether. Now he smiles. Now he comes to you for advice and more praise. And we all need praise...and we need it often. Kids thrive on it.

They are the David's in your class...small...poorly dressed...a loner...quiet...who doesn't want to call attention to himself. As the days progress, you pull up a chair beside him and attempt to strike up a conversation. You send him on errands and make a point to look at him as you are talking to the class.

The David's of the world may be slow and shy, but they will attempt to work their hearts out because you paid attention to them. And they are the ones who will bring you a little gift at Christmas that means everything because you know they couldn't afford even the simplest of gifts. Once in awhile, these kids will write a poem or an essay that will bring tears to your eyes, because their writing comes from the heart...misspelled words and all.

If kids you teach don't do anything else they will always surprise you. Often, the kids you least expect will return to tell you how much you meant to them when they were students. You may have forgotten them, but they certainly have not forgotten you. They usually say "I remember you said....." or "I have never forgotten that talk you had with me!" A teacher must never forget what he or she says may influence a young mind for years to come.

And if you are extremely lucky a student comes into your life that you will never forget. Thomas was such a student.

Thomas was small for his age...with short hair and bangs and big brown eyes full of sparkle and curiosity. He spoke very little broken English. How could I know the day he walked into my eighth grade computer class that he would capture my heart?

He had arrived in America the year before from Viet Nam, speaking no English, to live with a sister and brother. His mother was dead. His father and other siblings had remained in Viet Nam.

It didn't take long to discover that this diminutive young man was more eager to learn than any student I had ever taught. Thomas wanted to know everything! His first goal was to read, write and speak English correctly. At the same time, he wanted to excel in typing, computers, math, reading, science and the violin. And he did!

Thomas and I connected to each other immediately. He would convince his other teachers to allow him to come to my classroom during the day so I could help him with assignments or a personal problem he might be having. We worked and worked on his English. One day I told him to begin studying the dictionary because there he would find all the words he would ever need and what they meant. Sure enough, he bought himself a dictionary and began with the "A's." He kept me posted on his progress and what letter he was presently studying.

Thomas had one focus...to learn. He studied every minute he was at school and almost every minute he was at home — the exception being when he was asleep. He would call me often on the telephone to discuss whatever was bothering him or asking to give him an example of a new word he had learned but didn't understand.

Once he called to tell me that on his way back from the grocery store several kids had jumped him and beat the devil out of him. He didn't understand racial hatred in the America he loved.

When he became discouraged or frustrated with so much to learn, it was discouragement and frustration with himself. But with a small word of encouragement and a reminder of how far he had come in such a short time, he was up and running again...ready to conquer it all.

Thomas wanted more than anything to become an American and to fit in among everyone else. His dream was to become an American citizen. And I know he will.

I taught him to say in a Texas drawl, "I'm a Texan!" and "I'm in the oil bidness!" I would take his hand and off we would go to perform for other teachers. He is a delightful young man.

I shall never forget the day there was a knock on my classroom door and an invitation from the music teacher to step out into the hall for a surprise. There stood Thomas — violin in hand — who began to play the first piece of music he had learned. The sweet music brought others into the halls to listen while I stood there with goose-bumps and tears streaming down my face. It was a proud moment for Thomas...and me!

When the school year ended and throughout the summer, Thomas and I had long telephone conversations about his fear of going to high school. I would ask him to remember his fear when he came to America...his fear when be started school in a new country where he did not know the language...and his fear when he came to junior high school and how he had made it through with flying colors.

We talked about how he would be afraid when he went away to college...began his first job...and got married and had children because the unknown is scary until we experience it. I assured him that he would be fine and he could accomplish anything he wanted to throughout his life. You only had to tell Thomas something once. He never forgot it.

Thomas will graduate from high school in the spring of 1999. He will enter college with a major in pre-med and a minor in music. His dream is to become a heart surgeon. I have no doubt that his dream will become a reality. And who knows, that wonderful little boy with the bangs and big brown eyes may one day become as famous a heart surgeon as Dr. DeBakey or Dr. Cooley. It wouldn't surprise me at all. Thomas *will* make a difference in this world. He started at a disadvantage but never let that stop him. How fortunate I am to have been his teacher. And how proud he made me feel to be a teacher.

How badly do some students want an education? To answer this question consider Terlingua.

For twenty plus years high school students from the small town of Terlingua, Texas, rode a bus 160 miles round trip every week day to attend high school!

Climbing out of bed at 4:40 a.m., these students boarded the bus carrying their books, pillows and blankets. They slept on the way to school and often on the way back from school. In winter, they not only left in darkness, but also returned in darkness. Only to repeat the process again the next day. This is quite an accomplishment considering the number of students who can't get to school on time in their own home town, or often don't get there at all.

In August, 1997, Terlingua's own high school opened for the first time. The new school — built with grants and donations — is one of the smallest in Texas. And although the school had no library, cafeteria, gymnasium, foreign languages programs or the countless number of other special programs for special students, it *does* offer the opportunity for an education. Isn't that what schools were meant to provide?

Teachers are not looking for "perfect students," because they do not exist. There will always be students who are apathetic or will not do their homework, who have family problems that affect their schooling, who break-up with their first love and think the world is ending, who violate the dress code, who skip school and will sass a teacher on occasion.

Teachers are experienced in dealing with the normal problems of student behavior. But teaching should not be combat maneuvers. It should not be a constant problem solving arena of poor student behavior and disruptions. It should not be a situation of accountability for unrealistic expectations when students refuse to cooperate or learn.

Educators cannot take responsibility for the disintegration of the family unit in this country or ultimately for the disintegration of public schools, because they are not in control of either situation.

Anyone who believes that you can lead a horse to water but you cannot make him drink, must also firmly believe that you can send a student to school, but you cannot make him/her learn. Those students who encroach on the learning of others and will not take part in the learning process or those who are dangerous to others, do not belong in the public schools. These students should be removed and enrolled in a full-time alternative school for the remainder of the school year.

THERE SHOULD NOT BE A LONG LIST OF BUREAUCRATIC RED TAPE IN ORDER TO REMOVE A STUDENT

In the last few years we have all heard the trendy phrase Zero Tolerance in public schools. The public seems to think schools are operating under the umbrella of zero tolerance. The truth is Zero Tolerance does not exist, since there is too much red tape involved to remove a student. When teachers are subjected to verbal abuse *(which they often are)*, there are many steps to go through before anything can be done to remedy the situation. And many pages of documentation are required to document specific instances of abusive behavior. In fact, teachers are now sent to training on how to deal with verbal abuse in their classrooms.

To be perfectly frank, some administrators don't want to go to the trouble involved to remove a student. And what would they do with all those students anyway? Alternative schools and in-school suspension usually have no vacancies.

Zero Tolerance is just another catchy phrase to make things appear as if everything is running smoothly for students and teachers at school.

In the majority of cases, the same students are sent again and again to alternative school or in-school suspension...only to return to class to create the same problems again.

At the present, alternative school is no substitute for a regular classroom. Although teachers send assignments for students sent to alternative school or in-school suspension, the majority of students who get into enough trouble to be sent there didn't do their work while they were in their regular classes. They certainly don't intend to learn anything while in alternative school. These students who are gone for two or three weeks and later return to regular classes are even further behind all the other students. Some students are sent away for as long as a month or six weeks and then sent back to regular classes.

Nobody has ever addressed the issue of what a teacher is supposed to do with these students when they return to class. Usually, teachers end up baby-sitting them once again until their behavior becomes so unbearable the process is repeated and off they go to alternative school once again. *If* there is room for them.

There are students who simply cannot or will not function in a school where there are rules, dress codes, expectations of proper behavior, self-discipline and a work ethic of studying and learning.

When children are not raised in a structured home with rules and expectations, when they are ignorant of social rules that are made for the betterment of society, when they have not been taught to respect the rights of others, they will have problems conducting themselves properly in a school setting. Sadly, these are the kids we are seeing more and more today in our classrooms.

Public schools have tried, but failed to reshape the behavior and thinking of such students. While schools are still trying, they are still failing. This type of disruptive student population has rapidly increased during the last few years and continues to increase. Imagine the difficulty confronting a teacher who is trying to control and conduct a class with these disruptive students, plus all the others who are in the classroom.

Too many people feel these problems and concerns should remain the classroom teacher's problem. Others don't comprehend what a gigantic problem exist. And still others do not want to address the issue because they have no answers.

And then there are those who address the problems with solutions that only add to the problem. These are the ones who are in the position of making the rules and regulations for everybody to follow. And like the justice system, the rights of the perpetrators are protected...not the victim's rights.

If we are going to have Zero Tolerance, this means our tolerance for disruptive, destructive and dangerous behavior should be **zero, zilch, none, period...end of discussion.** And we have reached the point where we had better begin doing just that.

Repeat troublemakers should be required to be involved in some type of school or community service. Students have to learn that if they are going to break rules and infringe on the rights of others, they must suffer the consequences. However, this would be very difficult to achieve when students see how the athletic super stars get by with their unacceptable behavior as well as the common criminal.

Permanent alternative schools are long overdue. They should be places to try and educate students who have never learned to live by the rules, who have no regard for others and who refuse to believe that everyone needs a skill and/or an education. It is past the time when these troublemakers should be removed from their regular classes. These students should permanently be introduced to the other members of society who have the same views, but now reside in jails and prisons or on the streets or on welfare.

No doubt about it, such schools with effective programs would be expensive, but education has never been as expensive as ignorance. If something is not done to turn these kids around using a workable approach, they will become the future prison inmates, the homeless and the welfare recipients of tomorrow. What we spend on these educational programs today is certainly less expensive than what will be spent in the future. And what happens if they do not perform better in an alternative school? Why not have them sent to a juvenile boot camp?! This would give the courts an opportunity to do *their* part for education.

We do not owe students an apology when they are removed from public schools. But we should apologize to the taxpayers of the community who work hard to maintain a free public school system for those who want an education. Instead, we are forced to maintain a place for those who don't want an education and seriously hinder the learning process of those who do. Every man, woman and child in this nation should know and understand that the decay of intelligence, knowledge and order affects us all.

Some call it going back to the basics. I call it going back to square one, because in the last several years we have ignored some squares and skipped over some others. And in the process, we have added so many unnecessary squares that teachers are now playing a game of out-of-control **educational hopscotch.**

There is nothing wrong with trying new ways to teach if the old ways do not work. However, when students have not learned what is in the first few squares, jumping ahead is not the answer. We continue jumping around for this program and then jumping again to another program while leaping from one new educational approach to another. Then, we turn around and jump back to a previous square that seems all to familiar.

We leap over to this square because it's going to be the answer and then we jump over to another square because the last square was unworkable. The players *(read: teachers)* have jumped around so much they are dizzy and some don't even want to play anymore. Those who thought up the hopscotch game in the first place aren't even players. Here are a few suggestions for a new game of hopscotch...with fewer squares and some new rules in mind.

ALTERNATIVE SCHOOLS

Alternative schools should be available to accommodate students from middle school through high school and be **permanent for the entire school year**. The school should be available for students who have previously failed one or more grades or are consistent behavior problems — usually one in the same.

Although social promotion is not popular, a fourteen year old in the sixth grade is not a pretty picture. Nor is a sixteen year old in the eighth grade. What else can we do with these students but move them on...even though they don't know the academic basics for each grade?

The answer is that we should have a place for these repeaters with remediation courses available to them. Regular classroom teachers have "remediated" themselves into oblivion trying to get these students to pass.

Curriculum should be basically the same as regular school

with the addition of courses to help counsel these kids on drinking, drugs, violence, promiscuity and values.

In the past, the problems of our children and their childhood that concerned us the most was disease. Today, it is their destructive behavior and lack of knowledgeable skills.

Alternative schools should offer courses in vocational and computer education that would motivate these kids to become interested in learning a trade. "Eye Opener" courses should be offered to show them what their future holds without an education or a trade. Regular education — as it exist today — will not make an impression on these students...no matter how many programs we try.

There are so many professions that these students could explore with field trips to police academies, hospitals, newspapers, factories, technological schools, the courts and trades of all types. Students could be taught the education or training related to these professions.

Public schools are filled with students who will not graduate from high school. Teachers spend countless hours working with these "at risk" kids. Does it make a difference? Rarely.

Most teachers will tell you that these students are eventually passed on and will either drop out of school or be unable to read or comprehend their high school diploma. And a teacher's valuable time should be spent in the classroom on students who want to learn. Therefore, we should have an alternative way of teaching those who do not want to learn. It is time for change. Time for drastic changes.

BEGINNING AT THE BEGINNING: ELEMENTARY SCHOOLS

The elementary teacher provides the very foundation for all learning in the future of a child's life. These teachers with their overwhelming amount of responsibility are even less appreciated than their colleagues. Their job is an awesome one. The unpaid overtime they give to their profession is unbelievable.

Many elementary teachers arrive at school before 7:00 a.m. and leave anywhere between 5:30 and 7:30 p.m. What are they doing? Why do they stay so late?

Elementary teachers must have colorful new bulletin boards for every season and for every holiday and special event. Bulletin boards are time consuming and require new and different creative ideas. Colorful bulletin boards are *a requirement* and not a suggestion.

Student's work must be displayed. Every child's birthday must be acknowledged. Teachers must print all the papers they use for their students and create visuals for student motivation. And, of course, there is the never-ending grading of papers and posting grades in the gradebook or into the computer. Elementary kids want their graded papers returned *yesterday.* Therefore, papers must be graded daily — which is no small task.

Elementary teachers don't get away from their students for very long during the school day. They must escort their students every place they go. They walk them to and from physical education, music and art classes and to the library where they must supervise every move they make. They must walk their students to the cafeteria at lunch and wait in line with them until they are served and seated. A 30-minute duty free lunch for these teachers becomes a 15-minute duty free lunch...if they are lucky.

One example of "inclusion" in elementary schools is brought to life in this actual fourth grade class: three students are rolled into the classroom in wheelchairs each morning. All three are a Code 504 and none of them can communicate. They all have very low I.Q.'s. Their special code is known as Fragile X.

Accompanying the three students is their teacher and two aides who are with them as long as they are in school. (One adult is provided for each student.) The aides also roll into the classroom three COWS (computers on wheels). None of the three students can use the computers, but they go where the students go because it is the rule. How does one maneuver both a wheelchair and a COW? That's the teacher's and the aide's problem.

These students yell, scream and sometimes throw-up due to the excitement. They try to grab and bite the other students. The host regular teacher in this classroom must wait during the hour these three students are there to accomplish anything useful with the other students. Can learning possibly take place in such an atmosphere? The justification for inclusion is that these three students "need the socialization." But at what price and at whose cost?

This is only one incident of inclusion in today's public schools. There are many more types of disabled and handicapped children — on all levels of education — who are included in the public school arena. Some are not expected to learn, because they can't. They are there for "socialization" and because it is the law...should parents choose to have them there.

If this sounds heartless and cruel that teachers would prefer the "uneducable" not be mainstreamed into their classrooms, it is not. This is just one more unrealistic burden that has been thrown into the laps of teachers. And until you have walked in the shoes of a public school teacher, don't judge them!

Elementary schools should include grades one through six. The biggest mistake a school district ever made was including the sixth grade in middle school. Sixth graders are too small and too immature to be in middle school with seventh and eighth graders. It doesn't take a great deal of intelligence to figure this out *if* you know anything at all about public schools.

Repetitive instruction is the best technique for elementary school, but teachers say there is too much curriculum to cover to be very repetitive. They must teach the entire curriculum as well as all the things parents are not teaching their children. Elementary children must learn sharing, getting along with others and basic manners. And in today's world, this seems to be up to teachers to teach right from wrong and a host of other things once learned at home.

Elementary schools should be able to concentrate on reading, writing and arithmetic, as well as speaking and writing the English language...until students get it right. These subjects are so important that they should be taught over and over and over until they are mastered by every student. And if these subjects must be taught using what kids love...television, cartoon characters and computers to get results, then this should be used in the classroom.

If there is anything we know for sure, it is that if a child cannot read, write, calculate and communicate, he/she cannot do much of anything else. Yet, we still see students in junior and high school who cannot read...cannot write legibly...cannot spell...cannot write a complete sentence or a paragraph. They cannot do simple addition, subtraction, division and multiplication. And if a student hasn't learned the multiplication tables, forget trying to learn math.

Today, students are not learning the multiplication tables, because it involves study, effort and assistance at home.

AND THROW AWAY THE CALCULATORS IN ELEMENTARY

SCHOOL AND MIDDLE SCHOOL! KIDS MUST GO BACK TO THINKING AGAIN AND BE ABLE TO CALCULATE WITHOUT ME-CHANICAL HELP!

We should be able to teach a subject in elementary school and adequately determine through our own testing whether students have mastered the material. If they haven't, they shouldn't be allowed to advance. It's as simple as that. "You're going learn it, Sonny and Sally, and you're staying until you do!"

A classroom teacher should not suffer the punishment of having repeaters the next year. Talk about teacher burnout! Instead, these kids should be placed in remedial classes until the material is learned...for however long it takes.

Along with reading, writing and arithmetic, elementary teachers should teach values, citizenship, manners, hygiene, grooming and how to get along with others. If students do not learn these essential behaviors in elementary school, it is too late by the time they reach middle school or high school. Of course, if parents would do their job, these things would be learned at home where they belong. And time could be better spent by teachers on other matters.

Elementary school should include some history of the United States and an appreciation of our country. Add some art and creativity classes and elementary teachers have a full curriculum from kindergarten through sixth grade.

For the advanced students, a variety of mini-courses should be available. We cannot continue to hold back those who learn quickly with those who don't. Advanced courses in math, reading, writing and computer literacy are important to the curriculum. We should send students to middle school who can read and write well, calculate effectively, and who have some social values. Then, education can and will progress in a positive manner.

And what do we do with elementary troublemakers and those who make no effort to learn? A-L-T-E-R-N-A-T-I-V-E school! Yes, elementary teachers believe these students need one, too.

When teachers were asked what they would like the public to know about teaching from the trenches in elementary school, this is what they said:

"I am so frightened for the future of America. These kids know nothing when they come to school. We simply cannot teach them everything they should have learned from their parents. We are in deep trouble in this country." Gladys B.

"There is such a lack of support from administration. They will not follow through with disciplinary measures because, 'the parent is always right' and so they tell us, 'you take care of your own problems.'" Barbara M.

"There doesn't seem to be anybody with an ounce of common sense overseeing public school classrooms." Jackie R.

"One of the biggest jokes in public education today is Site-Based Decision Management. This is suppose to be decisions made by teachers in their school that will benefit their particular school. The truth is, it is ultimately what the principal wants and decides." Laurel R.

"I have taught school many years and recently I was asked by a new teacher why I was coloring Easter eggs, which I do every year with my fourth grade students. I tried to explain the value in the students reading directions, the application of those directions and the creativity involved. And last, but not least, kids will remember these types of things from their school days. They deserve some happy memories of school. I am relating this because I firmly believe that the teachers coming into the profession will not go to the trouble for the children that we always have. I am also not sure they understand what learning is all about. And I will let you in on a secret...these young new teachers will not stay in the profession long and we older experienced ones are leaving as fast as we can." Sally P.

"What I want the public to realize is that in kindergarten through fourth grade there is a cap of 22 students in each class. That looks great on paper, but beginning in the fifth grade, there are as many as 30 in a class. That is too many students for any one teacher and next to impossible to control. Then there is the lack of social values, the values that relate to poverty and ignorance, the "tough" ones, the English as a second language group and the gifted and talented and all those in between. We cannot do justice to anything or anybody because there are such varied needs. We are no longer requiring students to meet our expectations, but we are moving toward meeting

their expectations based on their limited knowledge and where they came from. The next stop is no expectations and bottom of the barrel standards." Billye S.

"*Like most teachers, I am sick and tired of attending inservices on "nothing." These are consistently a big waste of a teacher's time.*" Cynthia L.

"*The extra hours I devote to my students and my school are not appreciated. They are taken for granted. Just the time spent in the classroom every day is draining and very frustrating. I'm an excellent teacher and the children need me. However, I don't really believe I will stay in teaching.*" Margaret P.

MIDDLE SCHOOLS

Junior high or middle school is a crucial time in a youngster's life. It is a difficult and complex time and often a painful time. It is the time of awkwardness, peer cruelty, peer pressure and self-consciousness. And it is a time for rebellion, curiosity, maturity and immaturity.

Many believe that teachers of this age group should receive special combat pay! I'll vote for that!

During these years, students are living in a world of their own...often on a separate planet from the rest of us. Or at least it seems so. Hormones are cruising around their bodies and their attention span is from six to ten minutes. They are growing rapidly and they are either tired or full of more energy than an adult can ever remember having.

This group of kids believe they know everything, but in reality they know very little. They don't look beyond today and what feels good to them, nor do they worry about the consequences of tomorrow or next week or next year. Their heroes and role models scare the devil out of most of us. Values and attitudes have been molded and habits and behaviors are formed by this age.

At this age, it is a full-time job attempting to hold their interest and getting them to display a certain amount of effort...much less trying to teach them anything. Often, it is very much like trying to push an elephant that doesn't want to move. When you add those students who are lacking in values, acceptable attitudes and habits, and those who are dangerous and disruptive, a teacher of this age group feels like the elephant is winning and sitting squarely in the big middle of her/his back.

Somebody once said, "If you teach in junior high school, you are bordering on insanity!" If you weren't on the border of insanity when you started, you might be when you finish!

The ideal middle school consists of grades seven and eight. Social studies courses should focus on citizenship, pride, love of country and an appreciation for all of those who have fought for the freedoms they enjoy and take for granted. Children today do not have enough pride in being an American nor do they seem to care how much has been sacrificed for them by so many. And if they are ever going to have that pride and appreciation, how many places other than school will they learn it?

The contributions Steven Spielberg has made in bringing history to life in his movies is invaluable. His "Schendler's List" and "Saving Private Ryan" teaches more than any teacher or text book could accomplish.

English, math, communication courses, reading and writing must show a link to the tools needed to succeed in the work world. How these skills will help obtain upward mobility during a student's life should be demonstrated. Science, of course, is a must for any higher education.

Computer skills and technology courses are as important today as are all the other required courses.

Middle school is the time to begin simulating employment situations and showing students the importance of the skills they are learning and how this will relate when they finish school.

In business simulations, students should act as employees using their skills in math, English, reading, writing, spelling, communicating and computers. They should see first hand that employment hiring, advancement and dismissal is usually based on these skills...or lack of them.

Teachers have never understood why public schools have, for the most part, phased out vocational courses in middle school or to a large degree in high school. This is a mistake! A big mistake!

Every kid will not attend college. Every kid will not even finish high school. Yet we spend millions of dollars for "at risk" programs that do not include courses designed to keep kids interested in staying in school and in actually learning a trade.

Middle school kids are not like they were twenty years ago. If we don't find a way to reach them at this age, it isn't likely that we ever will. What is wrong with teaching them marketable skills? Students should be learning car repair and not car stealing. They should be learning to build and not destroy. There are many vocational courses for both girls and boys that could be developed to excite and interest them enough so they would want to learn more in high school.

Have you paid an electrician or a plumber lately? Do you know how much a bricklayer makes? How much are you willing to pay a good mechanic? How much do women pay a hair color specialist? How much would you be willing to pay someone who can "fix anything?" And the list goes on. We don't educate our kids to find out what they are good at doing and how they can make a good living doing it.

Students *must* begin to learn at this age what their life will be all about in the very near future. They must be made to realize that they have to equip themselves with marketable skills or prepare for a higher education. Family management courses should be required in junior and senior high schools that gives a realistic perspective on the cost of food, cars, insurance, utilities, rent/mortgage payments, child care, health care, clothes, entertainment, emergencies, credit and divorce. We desperately need a required course entitled "NOBODY WILL TAKE CARE OF YOU BUT YOU*!" (And forget about what all the politicians are saying!)*

We have to educate the future citizens of this country on the high cost of welfare, crime, drug abuse and disease. Students are never too young to begin learning these cold hard facts. After all, it is the tax paying citizens who must pay the bill for all of these things.

In view of the alarming increase in student dropouts and their disinterest in education, I used the following model for several years to demonstrate to my eighth grade students the reality of life and the necessity for an education and/or a marketable skill. Their interest, enthusiasm and amazement at what they learned proved to be highly successful. Even I was surprised. However, this business course is no longer available in middle school...another big mistake.

I include it here only to demonstrate just one of a dozen small ways we should be creating interest through the right curriculum. We cannot continue to do things in the same old tired way year after year. Times are too different and students are too sophisticated. And teachers cannot continue to spend their valuable time on preparing students for the standardized test when they could be preparing students for their future.

The following is an overview on how this could be accomplished.

Survival Simulation Model

Unit 1: Eighth grade students pretended they were tenth grade dropouts. They had to be completely self-supporting, because their parents refused to help them financially...except for making a small personal loan and co-signing a note.

Each student had to find a job that they were qualified to do and could realistically obtain. They read the want ads in the newspaper and had to call the place of employment to find the hourly wage. The job had to be approved by the teacher and certain guidelines were used in order to assure realistic employment.

Once the job was approved, each student had to figure their weekly and monthly wage (for a 40-hour week) with the appropriate deductions. *(What an eye-opener this was!)* "You mean after working that much, that's all the money I get?!" many of the students would complain.

Unit 2: Students were required to rent a furnished apartment they could afford with the deposit being paid by the personal loan from their parents, guardian or a relative. The loan was to be repaid in monthly installments. This loan also helped pay for kitchen staples and food needed to begin apartment living. Each student had the choice of having a roommate or living alone. *(Males lived with males and females with females. They quickly learned they couldn't afford to live alone.)*

Unit 3: Each student had to either buy a used car and purchase the necessary insurance, or they could ride the bus for transportation. Bus riders had to provide a bus schedule and figure the correct amount of money needed for the month. In order to purchase a car, each student had to have a parent or relative agree to co-sign their car loan. Otherwise, they had to hop a bus.

Monthly car and insurance payments had to be calculated. *(This was where the groaning and moaning started!)* "I can't even buy a decent car to drive, just an old ugly car!" "How can they make you buy insurance?" That explanation took an entire class period. One enterprising young lady decided to rent an apartment two blocks from work.

Unit 4: Students were given a list of monthly expenses to be subtracted from their net monthly salary. They were encouraged to go grocery shopping with a parent to get an education on food prices. They were required to buy enough food to include taking their lunch to work, unless they could show how they could eat out for lunch. *(The majority of students found out they had to "brown bag it"...just like their teachers!)* The students had fun making their menus for breakfast —"*Yes, you have to eat breakfast!*" — lunch and dinner. Most of them decided to buy the economy size peanut butter. They were required to make a list of food they would have to buy that would last until payday including the prices of the items.

Unit 5: Each student had to open a simulated checking account and write simulated checks for each of their monthly expenses. Of course, they had to keep a correct checkbook balance. It wasn't very long before several students were "in the red" and had written hot checks because their balance was incorrect. Now, they had to pay a large service charge to the bank for every bad check. *(What an impression this made!)* "What am I going to do now?" they asked. And I replied, "I don't know. You figure it out...you're on your own!" One student who was so caught up in the situation said to me, "But I never did want to quit school in the first place...but you made me do it and now look!"

Math skills were an extremely important part of this unit and it made a statement to these students that could not have been accomplished in any other way. As the days progressed, class discussions were held about the reality of living, working and paying bills. Eyes were opened, brains were thinking and reality became a part of their daily lives. But the realities of life were not over yet.

Unit 6: Students were given the opportunity to become aware of other realistic life situations when they each drew a slip of paper from the "LIFE ISN'T A BOWL OF CHERRIES BOX." Each slip of paper described their own personal problem that they had to deal with in an acceptable manner.

These problems included: the theft of their clothing during a break-in at their apartment, a six week illness that demanded rest and being off from work, a minor car accident which left them without transportation for several weeks, although they still had their car and insurance payments to make coupled with a bus expense, too.

Other problems they drew from the box: being laid-off from their job, the loss of their roommate and what that financial loss would mean, a week before payday and no food to eat, and a variety of other problems that life sometimes presents to us. The list is endless.

With a low paying job and no savings, students learned the cold hard facts of an inadequate education and no marketable job skills. They began the unit with excitement and enthusiasm and ended it with frustration and the realization of what it takes to prepare themselves for the real world. As one student so amply put it, "I had no idea life was like that!"

High school students tend to drop out at the ninth grade level, so the junior high years are a critical time. And the present curriculum does not recognize this fact.

HIGH SCHOOL

Have you talked to a high school teacher lately? They are leaving the profession as fast as they can or moving from one school district to another looking for a better teaching environment. However, for the most part, they find the same intolerable situations that all teachers face...the standardized testing craze...mounds of paperwork...over crowded classrooms...more and more responsibility, inadequate financial compensation and incompetent and non-supportive administrators. The most important reason is that many in the vast student population are discipline problems and refuse to learn. In addition, there are those who are inadequately prepared for high school.

There was a time when high school teachers blamed middle school teachers for a student's lack of skills when they reached high school. And middle school teachers placed the blame on elementary teachers when their students arrived with inadequate skills. Well, teachers don't do that anymore. Why? Simply stated, teachers finally realized they cannot perform miracles. However, the rest of society still holds public school teachers accountable for the uneducated students. And so in their defense, I cordially invite you to teach or substitute for a week in an elementary, middle or high school. Then, get back to me!

We should have two types of high schools — one for the college bound and one for vocational programs leading to marketable work skills. We *must* educate and train the blue-collar workers of this nation with an effective public school curriculum. If, after half a year in a vocational school, a student with good grades wishes to pursue a college program, he/she could transfer to the college bound high school. And those who are not making the grade in the college bound program could, in turn, transfer to the vocational school. There must be flexibility and the ability for students to be able to move between the programs.

We *must* educate the females of this nation who will not attend college to become self-sufficient and have the skills to support themselves and their children.

The time has come when we must teach a curriculum that will benefit the students who will never see the inside of a college or university.

We have to develop a curriculum that will maintain the interest of students who are considered at risk for dropping out. We should attempt to educate every single student in high school who is not college bound with a marketable skill. And students should not be able to graduate from high school until they have a skill. Will we reach every student? No, but we must make a better effort than what is being done now.

In the long run, it is much more important for a student who will never attend college to be able to support himself/herself than it is to be able to write a term paper, work an algebra problem, name all the capitals, dissect a frog, diagram a sentence, learn the symbols and atomic numbers of the periodic table, be able to recognize a polyhedron figure, or how many pizzas Americans would have to eat each week so that pizzas would form a line that wraps around the earth. Who cares?

And why do students need to know that the morning express train leaves the station with four cars, A, B, C, and D. D is the dining car and must always be between two of the cars, and therefore, be able to list all the ways the cars could be arranged. How many times will they run into this in their lives?

We have to teach students what is ahead, how to survive and what we all owe society. Every student should know the qualities employers are looking for: an education, computer skills, communication skills, problem solving skills and the ability to get along well with co-workers.

And most importantly, we must teach students to work at something they are good at doing and will enjoy doing. Our teenagers are less prepared for life than any other generation has ever been. They are so unprepared, it is terrifying to watch. Beginning in junior high school and continuing through high school, all changes in curriculum should reflect the needs of the students in the community. One plan will not benefit all schools and all students.

Teachers cannot change society anymore than they can change the world. However, they can make an impact on the lives of those children who depend on them to care about their needs. And teachers must teach and guide these children *realistically* towards the future. And they *must* teach these students well enough to make them understand the education they receive will determine the quality of their life...for the rest of their life.

FROM THE TRENCHES

"I discovered one day, several weeks into a new school year, that I only knew the names of a few of my students simply because I didn't have the time to learn the rest. The names I did know belonged to the trouble makers who consumed most of my time. Why do we continue to allow them to dominate our classrooms? Why do we even allow them in our classrooms?" Jack P.

"Our students have so many different needs and learning levels that a classroom has become a circus and I am the one attempting to do a balancing act that is impossible for one human being. And, I might add, I sure don't have a safety net! I am up there all alone." Elaine S.

"We have unrealistic expectations for today's teachers. We expect them to teach every student with the same curriculum and obtain the same results. It can't be done. The problems, needs and capabilities are too diverse. What is even more frustrating is that only teachers are smart enough to recognize that fact. The bureaucracy certainly isn't." Peter B.

There are millions of people in this nation earning a good living. There are millions earning an excellent living. None of these people were born with their knowledge and ability. They were taught by teachers. We don't hear much about these people. Instead, we hear about those who are not able to read, write, calculate or do much of anything else. And when we ask why, it is invariably stated that teachers are at fault.

Well, we can't have it both ways! Either we are educating our students or we are all sitting on our backsides doing nothing. The truth is — despite the overwhelming odds — public education is still alive. Teachers are working extremely hard and students are being educated. A good education is still available for every student who chooses to accept it. This is the best kept secret in America!

There is another best kept secret and that is teachers are worn down from all the students who don't care and from all the insane hopscotch ideas and programs the inane bureaucracy keeps throwing at them!

One day, the bureaucracy will throw and there will be nobody there to catch...at least no experienced catchers.

Chapter Eighteen
Especially For Teachers

ESPECIALLY FOR TEACHERS

Someone once remarked, "Line up a school faculty and give them each a gun and tell them to shoot themselves in the foot and they will!"

Some of them will surely ask, "How should we hold the gun? Should we shoot our right or left foot? Will we be tested afterwards? Should we document everything?"

And at least one or two will take detailed notes to be sure they have the correct instructions. It's also a safe bet that two or three others will be thinking about how a bulletin board might be done on the subject and what colors to use.

Ridiculous? Perhaps. But it does make a statement about teachers and the way they think and respond to what they are told to do...no matter how absurd it might be.

Teachers don't like it, but they are accustomed to being treated like elderly children and not the adults and professionals that they are. They have chronic "Student Syndrome." They are told what to teach and how to teach it in their classrooms — more often than not by those who are not teachers and don't know up from down about the subject. Teachers are treated much like students by the powers-that-be and that includes their administrators.

The most telling sign of this syndrome is that teachers either pass or fail professionally by the latest standardized test that reflects their students' overall test scores. Although teachers do not take the test, they receive a grade of pass or fail. Unlike their students, they have no control over the final outcome, but they are graded anyway. If test scores are up, teachers pass. If the scores are down, they fail.

Teachers' opinions are seldom sought, wanted or respected. Oh, they are put on committees and boards and what have you. And they are given survey after survey. When all is said and done, they are not even considered when important decisions are made, especially, when these decisions concern their welfare and professional abilities.

Teaching is very much like the military. The teaching troops are expected to keep their mouths shut and do as they are told. And above all, teachers must never rock the boat! They must row the boat and keep it afloat for everyone else. They can sit in the boat. They can stand in the boat. Nobody cares if they get pushed out of the boat or run over by the boat. But they cannot rock the boat. And those who do rock the boat are considered troublemakers. Furthermore, rock the boat by crossing an administrator — rightfully or wrongly — and swift punishment will follow. Administrators have many creative and subtle ways to punish those who rock the boat!

Consequently, the sad truth is teachers will gripe and moan and groan to each other about all the absurdities they are subjected to. However, they usually don't say or do anything constructive as a group to try and change or rectify the situation. They just leave the problems to fester and become more and more irritated and inflamed.

Are teachers wimps? Or do they just not care? Will we ever see them wise up and rise up? Your guess is as good as mine...but if I were a betting woman...I would probably bet against them taking a stand, at least before it is too late.

I personally have never seen five teachers agree on the same thing at the same time. And when they are asked to stand firm with others, their reply is usually, "I'm afraid to!" or "I can't afford to lose my job!" Therein lies one of the problems...is teaching just a job or is it a profession? A teacher never says, "I can't afford to lose my profession!"

And so teachers, this is for you...are you listening? *You are professionals!* It is time you acted like professionals!

Teachers, you must stand up...and stand up together to demand changes in our public schools. You owe it to the students and to yourselves. Perhaps you are the only ones who *can* save our public schools. One thing is for sure, you cannot continue to be apathetic toward your profession or the circumstances under which you are expected to teach.

There is a movement in this country for school choice. We continue to hear about the effective and productive charter schools, private schools and parochial schools. Then there is the voucher system where students can choose to attend a "good" school (high performing) as opposed to a "bad" school (low performing). And home schooling is growing by leaps and bounds.

What is the popularity of such schools? The answer is quite simple. Parents want their kids to get an education. And why are these schools successful and productive when public schools are not? It all boils down to the "D" word. and the "S" word. Discipline and Standards.

These schools expect and demand a certain standard of behavior and academic performance. If Joanie and Johnny can't follow the rules, they're out! Other advantages are smaller classes and very often entrance requirements. And most importantly, parents of these students want to raise their kids themselves and do not want the schools to raise them. The parents are not interested in schools being a social agency. They are interested in an educational agency.

My question is this: Why can't public schools be improved enough to be run the same way? Instead, schools have become the dumping ground for those whose parents do not want to raise their own children, but want the schools to do it for them. And public schools have become the safe haven for those who "can't" and those who "won't" conform to rules of discipline and standards of academic performance — let alone high academic performance.

Classes have become larger and standards have consistently been lowered. More and more programs are instituted to accommodate students who have mental, physical and academic problems, while the average and above average children get what time and energy their teachers have left over. And yet, we are still confused as to why public schools are sinking rapidly. But guess who is ultimately to blame? You know the answer to that one, **you are!**

Teachers, you must demand safe schools. You must accept nothing less than *genuine* zero tolerance for those students who should not be in the classroom. At present, zero tolerance is only two words that sound good, but don't mean anything. We already know that...and the students know it, too!

Local districts are afraid of lawsuits and sometimes rightly so. There are many parents just waiting for the opportunity to sue a school district for all sorts of strange reasons which they consider are "my child's rights." Additionally, zero tolerance never pertained to special needs students in the first place.

So, where does all this leave classroom teachers? It leaves them where they have always been...in the trenches, alone...fending for themselves while the administration chugs along with a business as usual attitude. Principals and vice principals have their hands tied, because they have little recourse in trying to remedy the situation. Who is going to back them? Central administration and local boards need to get their heads together and figure out where they will put those students who do not conform to discipline and standards. Otherwise, classrooms across this nation will soon be filled with first year teachers who will not remain and with those who are not qualified to teach...but are just warm bodies.

Not only are teachers attempting to teach under almost impossible circumstances, but they are also fighting a war by trying to do the job of an entire platoon with no weapons or ammunition. Teachers have to change this.

Teachers, if you would stand together, you could make your position heard in every local, state and federal election in this country. You have the capacity to put a stop to the insane idea that public schools should be all things to all people. And it is not the classroom teacher's responsibility to try and solve every social and educational problem thrown their way.

Politics and the education of students is a pathetic and losing combination at best. Since this is the system we have in this country, the least teachers can do is band together and elect individuals who are smart and caring enough to make the necessary changes so desperately needed. Yes, this is hard work. But teachers are used to hard work.

Teachers must find a way to upgrade the image of the profession and take part in the decision making processes regarding their profession. It is easy for others to issue illogical and excessive mandates for teachers to follow, since they don't have to follow them.

It is easy to schedule classes with thirty, forty or more students for one teacher to handle, because those who are in the position of hiring more teachers are not in the classroom.

And it is simple to demand "inclusion" for someone else to carry out. What could be easier than to expect teachers to manage, motivate and educate every single child — regardless of the situation or circumstance, as long as those making the rules do not have to carry them out?

The Supreme Court now has ruled that public schools must provide on-site health care for students. Who would have thought our schools also would become health care facilities?

Every teacher should recognize the enormous value of teaching and the importance of every teacher. Without teachers there would be no education in this nation. Think about that for a minute! Without you, education would come to a grinding halt!

Teachers, you are the ones who make all other professions possible. You are the backbone of this nation!

You are the ones who get down in the crowded trenches and push and shove, repeat and repeat, teach and re-teach, plead and hope, persist and persist, while taking criticism, abuse and constantly fighting disrespect. Through it all, you continue to try and motivate and encourage your students while receiving very little appreciation for any of the things you do. And no matter how much you do or how hard you try, the academic failure of a student and low test scores means *you* are held accountable. This is the reality for teachers today.

The general public has the mistaken idea that teachers are paid well, have small classes, leave the school at 3:30 p.m., have three months off in the summer and should certainly be able to produce high test scores and academic excellence with their students. Sounds like an ideal situation...if only it were true!

There isn't a person in education who should be making more than a classroom teacher! And if there was any justice in this world, a law would be passed tomorrow that required all the following people to teach school for three weeks a year. *(One week in kindergarten through elementary school...one week in middle school...and one week in high school)*

- Superintendents of schools
- Principals
- Local and state school board members
- All parents of students
- Every state and federal legislator
- Every governor in America

Talk about an eye-opener! What a shock this would be to their preconceived notions! Wouldn't this change education in a big hurry?

Well, there isn't any justice. None of that will happen, so the answers must come from another direction.

Let me be clear on one point. I **do not** advocate unions or collective bargaining of any kind for teachers for one simple reason...children are involved. I **do** advocate unity.

Unity...the fact or state of being one; accord; agreement; harmony. I can think of no profession that needs unity and solidarity more than the teaching profession.

Something is seriously wrong with a profession as important as teaching that has financial compensation so low a person cannot support his/her family without holding down a second job just to get by and make ends meet.

There is also something wrong with a profession that financially penalizes a person for years of experience while financially rewarding new recruits to attract them into the profession. This practice is backwards.

Paying signing bonuses to new teachers and paying extra financial compensation for special area teachers while ignoring the experienced and loyal teacher is unconscionable. And we sit on our fannies doing nothing about it.

Experienced teachers should be handsomely rewarded for each year they give to teaching, as well as rewarded for their experience and expertise. Teaching experience is the glue that holds the education system together. And teaching is a process that can be developed over years of doing just that: teaching.

The simple fact is most school districts know they have teachers who have taught anywhere from ten to thirty plus years in a vulnerable position. Not only have teachers invested their lives in their profession, they must also think about the money they have invested in their retirement pensions. And that is why salary increases become less and less over the years. Seems fair, doesn't it?

It is very strange to discover that almost without exception, new teachers coming into the profession have not researched what they will be making in terms of financial compensation in the years to come. They also have no idea how low their pensions will be at retirement.

More and more school districts are now encouraging teachers to retire early in order to hire less experienced teachers who are paid a lower salary. Experience doesn't seem to matter much anymore when a district can save a few bucks. Sounds like big business, doesn't it? In fact, some districts are offering a retirement package to encourage retirements with a lump sum percentage of a teacher's salary paid as an incentive. In these school districts, teachers are called "TWOfers." This means the school district can hire two new teachers out of college for the price of one experienced teacher.

When new teachers are the majority of a teaching faculty

and then leave the profession in three to five years, what happens then?

The time is quickly approaching when teachers in public schools with little or no experience will either just be coming into the profession or just going out. If the powers-that-be think there is a teacher shortage now, THEY "ain't seen 'nuthin yet!" And the endangered species, the experienced teacher, will only be a memory.

So what can *you* do to change things? You alone, can do very little. *All of you,* collectively, can move mountains. Many a teacher has fantasized about every teacher in America calling in sick for a day. And that is all it is...a fantasy. But the effects of such a day would be overwhelming!

You can insist on adequate salaries, good benefits and a retirement system that rewards you handsomely for your years of service.

Teachers are the most uninformed populace when it comes to bills that are introduced that could affect them or their retirement and benefits package.

Teachers, together you can put a stop to the madness of trying to solve the multitude of social problems that have been dropped in your laps.

You are not baby-sitters and shouldn't be expected to baby-sit students.

You are not abusers, but you are often abused both verbally and physically.

You are not members of law enforcement, but you are expected to control parolees and police those who are dangerous. And you are expected to teach effectively while trying to keep your students and yourself safe at the same time.

Although you may not be a special education teacher or special needs teacher, you are teaching these students anyway. Slowly, over time, you have become a special education teacher whether you wanted to or not.

You are not multilingual, but you must teach the multilingual.

You do everything humanly possible to prepare your students for the TEST and then you are blamed if students give a poor showing. This is not *your* fault! This is the *student's* fault. You are not a magician, but you are expected to be magical. And if you haven't heard, THEY have decided THE TEST is now too easy.

How do you show accountability? You show it every day you are in the classroom. And if you do not, then you shouldn't be there. You wear multiple hats trying to be all things to all people, but the smallest hat you wear today seems to be the one just for actual teaching. As all teachers know, the majority of their time is spent on discipline, preparing for THE TEST and mounds of paperwork.

Teachers must learn to say the words, "No! Enough is enough!"

One of the most wonderful things about being an American is freedom of speech. We teach this freedom to our students, but we seem to forget we also have the right to express our views and to speak out for what we think is just and right. Teachers are Americans, too! They are taxpaying Americans! Has everybody forgotten this along the way?

Some teachers who read this book cannot identify with some of the serious problems discussed. If this is the case, you are very fortunate indeed. Other teachers face even greater problems than those that have been addressed. However, all teachers can identify with the social problems, unrealistic teaching demands, the massive amounts of unnecessary paperwork and the testing craze that has taken on a life of its own and is out of control.

Teachers can all identify with overcrowded classes, inadequate supplies, impossible student behavior, disrespect and the frustration and anger felt toward the people making decisions for the profession. Perhaps those who don't have the vaguest idea of what is going on in the classroom don't really care, but teachers should!

Public education has become a social agency and our job is to solve social problems.

All of us are fully aware of the political football games played using teachers as the footballs. This is called scapegoat football. And the Super Bowl is held each year during THE TEST. We hear the disrespect and criticism of our profession and we have no way to compete in the game or to fight back. **Or do we?**

Teachers have become the scapegoats for the ills of our society — plain and simple. If students are dropping out of school it's due to the ineffectiveness of teachers. When students cannot read, teachers are not doing their job. If students are behavior problems in the classroom, the teacher is at fault because she/he cannot control students.

The bottom line is students are not held responsible for their own choices and actions. Parents are not held responsible for their own children's choices and actions. Only teachers are held responsible. How can this make sense to anybody?

I personally have known teachers who have left a parent conference in tears after the parents yelled, screamed and cursed them. This is not acceptable behavior toward any teacher. Ditto when any administrator does the same thing.

Teachers, you will never sign million dollar contracts or endorse products for television commercials. You will receive few awards or little recognition for your work. And that is all right. Nobody expects this.

You will never receive stock options, expense accounts, Christmas bonuses, country club memberships or a long and leisurely lunch hour. And that's all right, too. Because teachers have common sense they know and accept this. Benefits and perks are out of the realm of possibility.

However, teachers should earn enough to support their families and support them well. They deserve adequate compensation for their years of teaching experience. Major raises should focus on the experienced and not the inexperienced teacher. Those coming into the profession should also be paid handsomely. As we all know, teachers more than earn every dime that they are paid!

At retirement every teacher should have financial security. It is a national disgrace for states to send teachers into retirement with pensions so low that they are at or slightly above the poverty level. This in itself says how much regard we have for American teachers.

Why should we as a nation show our teachers a deep respect and why should we financially reward them with high incomes? For those who don't have an answer, read on...

Teachers will touch and influence the lives of thousands of young people during their years in the classroom.

Teachers will serve as a role model for morals, values, citizenship and patriotism while attempting to build respect for self-worth and developing a curiosity and thirst for learning in their students.

Teachers take our most precious raw material and work diligently to help shape and mold that precious material into citizens who will literally determine the survival of our nation. They attempt to do this with every young person they come into contact with in schools across this country. Very often, they are successful. Sometimes, they are unsuccessful. But what an awesome responsibility! What an awesome profession!

And in the maze and haze of all the responsibility, distractions and unreasonable demands, teachers continue to teach with their hands tied. They always have and they always will try to educate students to the best of their ability for as long as they are in the trenches. This is what they do. This is who they are.

Teachers, if you want change you must stand together as one. To accomplish this, you must begin linking together in your respective schools by supporting each other. You must attend school board meetings and let your voices be heard.

Additionally, you should be active in all local, state and national elections. Only then can you be a positive force to be reckoned with.

You must unite with other schools in the community and then join together with state-wide groups in a united support system and begin speaking out. How can you accomplish such a thing?

Every school should elect a delegate. Every delegate should meet state-wide and then join with all the other states with a common purpose, to educate young people, to have the best schools staffed with respected professionals who are allowed to use their individual talents, to have administrators who are supportive leaders, to have absolute zero tolerance with alternative schooling for problem students, a curriculum designed to accommodate the present and the future, a method of testing that is productive and not counterproductive, and financial compensation that is in line with other professions of vital importance.

And lastly, if teachers do not put an end to the insane idea that they should be held accountable for the performance of every student who walks into their classroom — regardless of the students ability, inability or behavior over which they have no control — then we deserve everything that is thrown at us in the future. If teachers continue to shoot themselves in the foot without speaking up for themselves, then this is their choice.

Teachers, we have not been supportive of one another in the past. We may have different ideas and opinions, but we are all ultimately trying to go in the same direction and accomplish the same thing. We don't like change, but life is change and we can't get around it. And if anything needs changing, it is cer-

215

tainly our public schools and our profession!

To win the war we are fighting in the trenches, we must go together into the future. Otherwise, we are collectively "just giving ourselves a zero!"

I want to close with a quotation sent to me from a teacher. Its deeply significant message says it all:

"I once saw some graffiti written on the Berlin Wall. It was a message to all Berliners. Roughly translated it said, 'LIKE A SINGLE TREE, STAND TALL, STAND STRAIGHT, STAND FREE, BUT DO NOT FORGET THE BROTHERHOOD OF THE FOREST.' I think this has a message to all of us who believe in our profession, in each other and in public education."

About the Author

Mary Jack Edwards was born and reared in the Big Bend area of Marfa, Texas — home of the Marfa lights.

The mother of two sons, Paul and Christopher Ingle, and the grandmother of Ryan and Taylor, she has been a public school teacher for the past thirty-one years. She resides in Irving, Texas.

THE END IS HERE!

Now that you have finished this book on what is right, wrong and needs attention by public education institutions across the nation, do your part. Send a copy to a teaching friend, school board member, legislator, taxpayer, or concerned parent.

Complete this order form and help spread the word!

Send _____ copies @ $19.95 each, plus $2.30 shipping and

handling for a total of _____ to:

Name: _____

Address: _____

City/State/Zip: _____

Mail your order and payment to:

Ringtail Productions Limited
P.O. Box 141084
Irving, TX 75014

If you are a business that would like to be considered as a marketing partner with exclusive ordering and price discounts, contact the publisher: Ringtail Productions Limited, at the above address, or e-mail: **mehoward@airmail.net**